Abolitionist Poems Of John Greenleaf Whittier

John Greenleaf Whittier was born December 17, 1807, in Haverhill, Massachusetts. Growing up on the family farm his education was little and informal. He first published in 1826 before attending Haverhill Academy from 1827 to 1828, supporting himself as a shoemaker and schoolteacher. By age twenty, his published verse had brought him to the attention of the antislavery cause. A Quaker, Whittier worked passionately for abolitionist newspapers and magazines. He was active in support of National Republican candidates he himself became a delegate in 1831 to the national Republican Convention in support of Henry Clay. In 1832 he ran for Congress but was unsuccessful.

Legends Of New England In Prose And Verse, was published in 1831 followed in 1833 by *Justice and Expedience* which urged immediate abolition. In 1834 he was elected as a Whig for one term to the Massachusetts legislature. The following year he mobbed and stoned in Concord, New Hampshire before moving in 1836 to Amesbury, Massachusetts, where he worked for the American Anti-Slavery Society. During his editorship of the Pennsylvania Freeman, in May 1838, the paper's offices were burned to the ground and sacked during the destruction of Pennsylvania Hall by a mob.

Whittier founded the antislavery Liberty party in 1840 and ran for Congress in 1842. In the mid-1850s he began to work for the formation of the Republican party; supporting the presidential candidacy of John C. Frémont in 1856. He helped to found Atlantic Monthly in 1857. Although Whittier was close friends with Elizabeth Lloyd Howell and considered marrying her, in 1859 he decided against it.

Whittier supporters would never claim he was a poet of the first rank but all would concede that his poems on abolition give him a vaunted place for those efforts.

With the end of the civil war his work changed course and in 1866 he published what would prove to be his most popular collection *Snow Bound*. With this he became the most popular of the Fireside poets.

John Greenleaf Whittier died at Hampton falls, New Hampshire on 7th September 1892.

Index Of Poems

A Greeting

Thrice welcome from the Land of Flowers
And golden-fruited orange bowers
To this sweet, green-turfed June of ours!
To her who, in our evil time,
Dragged into light the nation's crime
With strength beyond the strength of men,
And, mightier than their swords, her pen!
To her who world-wide entrance gave
To the log-cabin of the slave;
Made all his wrongs and sorrows known,
And all earth's languages his own,
North, South, and East and West, made all
The common air electrical,
Until the o'ercharged bolts of heaven
Blazed down, and every chain was riven!

Welcome from each and all to her
Whose Wooing of the Minister
Revealed the warm heart of the man
Beneath the creed-bound Puritan,
And taught the kinship of the love
Of man below and God above;
To her whose vigorous pencil-strokes
Sketched into life her Oldtown Folks;
Whose fireside stories, grave or gay,
In quaint Sam Lawson's vagrant way,
With old New England's flavor rife,
Waifs from her rude idyllic life,
Are racy as the legends old
By Chaucer or Boccaccio told;
To her who keeps, through change of place
And time, her native strength and grace,
Alike where warm Sorrento smiles,
Or where, by birchen-shaded isles,
Whose summer winds have shivered o'er

The icy drift of Labrador,
She lifts to light the priceless Pearl
Of Harpswell's angel-beckoned girl!
To her at threescore years and ten
Be tributes of the tongue and pen;
Be honor, praise, and heart-thanks given,
The loves of earth, the hopes of heaven!

Ah, dearer than the praise that stirs
The air to-day, our love is hers!
She needs no guaranty of fame
Whose own is linked with Freedom's name.
Long ages after ours shall keep
Her memory living while we sleep;
The waves that wash our gray coast lines,
The winds that rock the Southern pines,
Shall sing of her; the unending years
Shall tell her tale in unborn ears.
And when, with sins and follies past,
Are numbered color-hate and caste,
White, black, and red shall own as one
The noblest work by woman done.

A Sabbath Scene
Scarce had the solemn Sabbath-bell
Ceased quivering in the steeple,
Scarce had the parson to his desk
Walked stately through his people,
When down the summer-shaded street
A wasted female figure,
With dusky brow and naked feet,
Came rushing wild and eager.
She saw the white spire through the trees,
She heard the sweet hymn swelling:
O pitying Christ! a refuge give
The poor one in Thy dwelling!
Like a scared fawn before the hounds,
Right up the aisle she glided,
While close behind her, whip in hand,
A lank-haired hunter strided.
She raised a keen and bitter cry,
To Heaven. and Earth appealing;
Were manhood's generous pulses dead?
Had woman's heart no feeling?
A score of stout hands rose between
The hunter and the flying:
Age clenched his staff, and maiden eyes
Flashed tearful, yet defying.
'Who dares profane this house and day?'
Cried out the angry pastor.
'Why, bless your soul, the wench's a slave,

And I'm her lord and master!
'I've law and gospel on my side,
And who shall dare refuse me?'
Down came the parson, bowing low,
'My good sir, pray excuse me!
'Of course I know your right divine
To own and work and whip her;
Quick, deacon, throw that Polyglott
Before the wench, and trip her!'
Plump dropped the holy tome, and o'er
Its sacred pages stumbling,
Bound hand and foot, a slave once more,
The hapless wretch lay trembling.
I saw the parson tie the knots,
The while his flock addressing,
The Scriptural claims of slavery
With text on text impressing.
'Although,' said he, 'on Sabbath day
All secular occupations
Are deadly sins, we must fulfil
Our moral obligations:
'And this commends itself as one
To every conscience tender;
As Paul sent back Onesimus,
My Christian friends, we send her!'
Shriek rose on shriek, the Sabbath air
Her wild cries tore asunder;
I listened, with hushed breath, to hear
God answering with his thunder!
All still! the very altar's cloth
Had smothered down her shrieking,
And, dumb, she turned from face to face,
For human pity seeking!
I saw her dragged along the aisle,
Her shackles harshly clanking;
I heard the parson, over all,
The Lord devoutly thanking!
My brain took fire: 'Is this,' I cried,
'The end of prayer and preaching?
Then down with pulpit, down with priest,
And give us Nature's teaching!
'Foul shame and scorn be on ye all
Who turn the good to evil,
And steal the Bible from the Lord,
To give it to the Devil!
'Than garbled text or parchment law
I own a statute higher;
And God is true, though every book
And every man's a liar!'
Just then I felt the deacon's hand
In wrath my coat-tail seize on;
I heard the priest cry, 'Infidel!'

The lawyer mutter, 'Treason!'
I started up, where now were church,
Slave, master, priest, and people?
I only heard the supper-bell,
Instead of clanging steeple.
But, on the open window's sill,
O'er which the white blooms drifted,
The pages of a good old Book
The wind of summer lifted,
And flower and vine, like angel wings
Around the Holy Mother,
Waved softly there, as if God's truth
And Mercy kissed each other.
And freely from the cherry-bough
Above the casement swinging,
With golden bosom to the sun,
The oriole was singing.
As bird and flower made plain of old
The lesson of the Teacher,
So now I heard the written Word
Interpreted by Nature!
For to my ear methought the breeze
Bore Freedom's blessed word on;
Thus saith the Lord: Break every yoke,
Undo the heavy burden!

A Song For The Time

Up, laggards of Freedom! our free flag is cast
To the blaze of the sun and the wings of the blast;
Will ye turn from a struggle so bravely begun,
From a foe that is breaking, a field that's half won?
Whoso loves not his kind, and who fears not the Lord,
Let him join that foe's service, accursed and abhorred!
Let him do his base will, as the slave only can,
Let him put on the bloodhound, and put off the Man!
Let him go where the cold blood that creeps in his veins
Shall stiffen the slave-whip, and rust on his chains;
Where the black slave shall laugh in his bonds, to behold
The White Slave beside him, self-lettered and sold!
But ye, who still boast of hearts beating and warm,
Rise, from lake shore and ocean's, like waves in a storm,
Come, throng round our banner in Liberty's name,
Like winds from your mountains, like prairies aflame!
Our foe, hidden long in his ambush of night,
Now, forced from his covert, stands black in the light.
Oh, the cruel to Man, and the hateful to God,
Smite him down to the earth, that is cursed where he trod!
For deeper than thunder of summer's loud shower,
On the dome of the sky God is striking the hour!
Shall we falter before what we're prayed for so long,
When the Wrong is so weak, and the Right is so strong?

Come forth all together! come old and come young,
Freedom's vote in each hand, and her song on each tongue;
Truth naked is stronger than Falsehood in mail;
The Wrong cannot prosper, the Right cannot fail!
Like leaves of the summer once numbered the foe,
But the hoar-frost is falling, the northern winds blow;
Like leaves of November erelong shall they fall,
For earth wearies of them, and God's over all!

Abolition Of Slavery In The District Of Columbia, 1862

When first I saw our banner wave
Above the nation's council-hall,
I heard beneath its marble wall
The clanking fetters of the slave!
In the foul market-place I stood,
And saw the Christian mother sold,
And childhood with its locks of gold,
Blue-eyed and fair with Saxon blood.
I shut my eyes, I held my breath,
And, smothering down the wrath and shame
That set my Northern blood aflame,
Stood silent, where to speak was death.
Beside me gloomed the prison-cell
Where wasted one in slow decline
For uttering simple words of mine,
And loving freedom all too well.
The flag that floated from the dome
Flapped menace in the morning air;
I stood a perilled stranger where
The human broker made his home.
For crime was virtue: Gown and Sword
And Law their threefold sanction gave,
And to the quarry of the slave
Went hawking with our symbol-bird.
On the oppressor's side was power;
And yet I knew that every wrong,
However old, however strong,
But waited God's avenging hour.
I knew that truth would crush the lie,
Somehow, some time, the end would be;
Yet scarcely dared I hope to see
The triumph with my mortal eye.
But now I see it! In the sun
A free flag floats from yonder dome,
And at the nation's hearth and home
The justice long delayed is done.
Not as we hoped, in calm of prayer,
The message of deliverance comes,
But heralded by roll of drums
On waves of battle-troubled air!
Midst sounds that madden and appall,

The song that Bethlehem's shepherds knew!
The harp of David melting through
The demon-agonies of Saul!
Not as we hoped; but what are we?
Above our broken dreams and plans
God lays, with wiser hand than man's,
The corner-stones of liberty.
I cavil not with Him: the voice
That freedom's blessed gospel tells
Is sweet to me as silver bells,
Rejoicing! yea, I will rejoice!
Dear friends still toiling in the sun;
Ye dearer ones who, gone before,
Are watching from the eternal shore
The slow work by your hands begun,
Rejoice with me! The chastening rod
Blossoms with love; the furnace heat
Grows cool beneath His blessed feet
Whose form is as the Son of God!
Rejoice! Our Marah's bitter springs
Are sweetened; on our ground of grief
Rise day by day in strong relief
The prophecies of better things.
Rejoice in hope! The day and night
Are one with God, and one with them
Who see by faith the cloudy hem
Of Judgment fringed with Mercy's light

Aechdeacon Barbour
Through the long hall the shuttered windows shed
A dubious light on every upturned head;
On locks like those of Absalom the fair,
On the bald apex ringed with scanty hair,
On blank indifference and on curious stare;
On the pale Showman reading from his stage
The hieroglyphics of that facial page;
Half sad, half scornful, listening to the bruit
Of restless cane-tap and impatient foot,
And the shrill call, across the general din,
'Roll up your curtain! Let the show begin!'
At length a murmur like the winds that break
Into green waves the prairie's grassy lake,
Deepened and swelled to music clear and loud,
And, as the west-wind lifts a summer cloud,
The curtain rose, disclosing wide and far
A green land stretching to the evening star,
Fair rivers, skirted by primeval trees
And flowers hummed over by the desert bees,
Marked by tall bluffs whose slopes of greenness show
Fantastic outcrops of the rock below;
The slow result of patient Nature's pains,

And plastic fingering of her sun and rains;
Arch, tower, and gate, grotesquely windowed hall,
And long escarpment of half-crumbled wall,
Huger than those which, from steep hills of vine,
Stare through their loopholes on the travelled Rhine;
Suggesting vaguely to the gazer's mind
A fancy, idle as the prairie wind,
Of the land's dwellers in an age unguessed;
The unsung Jotuns of the mystic West.
Beyond, the prairie's sea-like swells surpass
The Tartar's marvels of his Land of Grass,
Vast as the sky against whose sunset shores
Wave after wave the billowy greenness pours;
And, onward still, like islands in that main
Loom the rough peaks of many a mountain chain,
Whence east and west a thousand waters run
From winter lingering under summer's sun.
And, still beyond, long lines of foam and sand
Tell where Pacific rolls his waves a-land,
From many a wide-lapped port and land-locked bay,
Opening with thunderous pomp the world's highway
To Indian isles of spice, and marts of far Cathay.
'Such,' said the Showman, as the curtain fell,
'Is the new Canaan of our Israel;
The land of promise to the swarming North,
Which, hive-like, sends its annual surplus forth,
To the poor Southron on his worn-out soil,
Scathed by the curses of unnatural toil;
To Europe's exiles seeking home and rest,
And the lank nomads of the wandering West,
Who, asking neither, in their love of change
And the free bison's amplitude of range,
Rear the log-hut, for present shelter meant,
Not future comfort, like an Arab's tent.'
Then spake a shrewd on-looker, 'Sir,' said he,
'I like your picture, but I fain would see
A sketch of what your promised land will be
When, with electric nerve, and fiery-brained,
With Nature's forces to its chariot chained,
The future grasping, by the past obeyed,
The twentieth century rounds a new decade.'
Then said the Showman, sadly: 'He who grieves
Over the scattering of the sibyl's leaves
Unwisely mourns. Suffice it, that we know
What needs must ripen from the seed we sow;
That present time is but the mould wherein
We cast the shapes of holiness and sin.
A painful watcher of the passing hour,
Its lust of gold, its strife for place and power;
Its lack of manhood, honor, reverence, truth,
Wise-thoughted age, and generous-hearted youth;
Nor yet unmindful of each better sign,

The low, far lights, which on th' horizon shine,
Like those which sometimes tremble on the rim
Of clouded skies when day is closing dim,
Flashing athwart the purple spears of rain
The hope of sunshine on the hills again:
I need no prophet's word, nor shapes that pass
Like clouding shadows o'er a magic glass;
For now, as ever, passionless and cold,
Doth the dread angel of the future hold
Evil and good before us, with no voice
Or warning look to guide us in our choice;
With spectral hands outreaching through the gloom
The shadowy contrasts of the coming doom.
Transferred from these, it now remains to give
The sun and shade of Fate's alternative.'
Then, with a burst of music, touching all
The keys of thrifty life, the mill-stream's fall,
The engine's pant along its quivering rails,
The anvil's ring, the measured beat of flails,
The sweep of scythes, the reaper's whistled tune,
Answering the summons of the bells of noon,
The woodman's hail along the river shores,
The steamboat's signal, and the dip of oars:
Slowly the curtain rose from off a land
Fair as God's garden. Broad on either hand
The golden wheat-fields glimmered in the sun,
And the tall maize its yellow tassels spun.
Smooth highways set with hedge-rows living green,
With steepled towns through shaded vistas seen,
The school-house murmuring with its hive-like swarm,
The brook-bank whitening in the grist-mill's storm,
The painted farm-house shining through the leaves
Of fruited orchards bending at its eaves,
Where live again, around the Western hearth,
The homely old-time virtues of the North;
Where the blithe housewife rises with the day,
And well-paid labor counts his task a play.
And, grateful tokens of a Bible free,
And the free Gospel of Humanity,
Of diverse sects and differing names the shrines,
One in their faith, whate'er their outward signs,
Like varying strophes of the same sweet hymn
From many a prairie's swell and river's brim,
A thousand church-spires sancify the air
Of the calm Sabbath, with their sign of prayer.
Like sudden nightfall over bloom and green
The curtain dropped: and, momently, between
The clank of fetter and the crack of thong,
Half sob, half laughter, music swept along;
A strange refrain, whose idle words and low,
Like drunken mourners, kept the time of woe;
As if the revellers at a masquerade

Heard in the distance funeral marches played.
Such music, dashing all his smiles with tears,
The thoughtful voyager on Ponchartrain hears,
Where, through the noonday dusk of wooded shores
The negro boatman, singing to his oars,
With a wild pathos borrowed of his wrong
Redeems the jargon of his senseless song.
'Look,' said the Showman, sternly, as he rolled
His curtain upward. 'Fate's reverse behold!'
A village straggling in loose disarray
Of vulgar newness, premature decay;
A tavern, crazy with its whiskey brawls,
With 'Slaves at Auction!' garnishing its walls;
Without, surrounded by a motley crowd,
The shrewd-eyed salesman, garrulous and loud,
A squire or colonel in his pride of place,
Known at free fights, the caucus, and the race,
Prompt to proclaim his honor without blot,
And silence doubters with a ten-pace shot,
Mingling the negro-driving bully's rant
With pious phrase and democratic cant,
Yet never scrupling, with a filthy jest,
To sell the infant from its mother's breast,
Break through all ties of wedlock, home, and kin,
Yield shrinking girlhood up to graybeard sin;
Sell all the virtues with his human stock,
The Christian graces on his auction-block,
And coolly count on shrewdest bargains driven
In hearts regenerate, and in souls forgiven!
Look once again! The moving canvas shows
A slave plantation's slovenly repose,
Where, in rude cabins rotting midst their weeds,
The human chattel eats, and sleeps, and breeds;
And, held a brute, in practice, as in law,
Becomes in fact the thing he's taken for.
There, early summoned to the hemp and corn,
The nursing mother leaves her child new-born;
There haggard sickness, weak and deathly faint,
Crawls to his task, and fears to make complains;
And sad-eyed Rachels, childless in decay,
Weep for their lost ones sold and torn away!
Of ampler size the master's dwelling stands,
In shabby keeping with his half-tilled lands;
The gates unhinged, the yard with weeds unclean,
The cracked veranda with a tipsy lean.
Without, loose-scattered like a wreck adrlft,
Signs of misrule and tokens of unthrift;
Within, profusion to discomfort joined,
The listless body and the vacant mind;
The fear, the hate, the theft and falsehood, born
In menial hearts of toil, and stripes, and scorn!
There, all the vices, which, like birds obscene,

Batten on slavery loathsome and unclean,
From the foul kitchen to the parlor rise,
Pollute the nursery where the child-heir lies,
Taint infant lips beyond all after cure,
With the fell poison of a breast impure;
Touch boyhood's passions with the breath of flame,
From girlhood's instincts steal the blush of shame.
So swells, from low to high, from weak to strong,
The tragic chorus of the baleful wrong;
Guilty or guiltless, all within its range
Feel the blind justice of its sure revenge.
Still scenes like these the moving chart reveals.
Up the long western steppes the blighting steals;
Down the Pacific slope the evil Fate
Glides like a shadow to the Golden Gate:
From sea to sea the drear eclipse is thrown,
From sea to sea the Mauvaises Terres have grown,
A belt of curses on the New World's zone!
The curtain fell. All drew a freer breath,
As men are wont to do when mournful death
Is covered from their sight. The Showman stood
With drooping brow in sorrow's attitude
One moment, then with sudden gesture shook
His loose hair back, and with the air and look
Of one who felt, beyond the narrow stage
And listening group, the presence of the age,
And heard the footsteps of the things to be,
Poured out his soul in earnest words and free.
'O friends!' he said, 'in this poor trick of paint
You see the semblance, incomplete and faint,
Of the two-fronted Future, which, to-day,
Stands dim and silent, waiting in your way.
To-day, your servant, subject to your will;
To-morrow, master, or for good or ill.
If the dark face of Slavery on you turns,
If the mad curse its paper barrier spurns,
If the world granary of the West is made
The last foul market of the slaver's trade,
Why rail at fate? The mischief is your own.
Why hate your neighbor? 'Blame yourselves alone!
'Men of the North! The South you charge with wrong
Is weak and poor, while you are rich and strong.
If questions, — idle and absurd as those
The old-time monks and Paduan doctors chose,
Mere ghosts of questions, tariffs, and dead banks,
And scarecrow pontiffs, never broke your ranks,
Your thews united could, at once, roll back
The jostled nation to its primal track.
Nay, were you simply steadfast, manly, just,
True to the faith your fathers left in trust,
If stainless honor outweighed in your scale
A codfish quintal or a factory bale,

Full many a noble heart, (and such remain
In all the South, like Lot in Siddim's plain,
Who watch and wait, and from the wrong's control
Keep white and pure their chastity of soul,)
Now sick to loathing of your weak complaints,
Your tricks as sinners, and your prayers as saints,
Would half-way meet the frankness of your tone,
And feel their pulses beating with your own,
'The North! the South! no geographic line
Can fix the boundary or the point define,
Since each with each so closely interblends,.
Where Slavery rises, and where Freedom ends.
Beneath your rocks the roots, far-reaching, hide
Of the fell Upas on the Southern side;
The tree whose branches in your northwinds wave
Dropped its young blossoms on Mount Vernon's grave;
The nursling growth of Monticello's crest
Is now the glory of the free Northwest;
To the wise maxims of her olden school
Virginia listened from thy lips, Rantoul;
Seward's words of power, and Sumner's fresh renown,
Flow from the pen that Jefferson laid down!
And when, at length, her years of madness o'er,
Like the crowned grazer on Euphrates' shore,
From her long lapse to savagery, her mouth
Bitter with baneful herbage, turns the South,
Resumes her old attire, and seeks to smooth
Her unkempt tresses at the glass of truth,
Her early faith shall find a tongue again,
New Wythes and Pinckneys swell that old refrain,
Her sons with yours renew the ancient pact,
The myth of Union prove at last a fact!
Then, if one murmur mars the wide content,
Some Northern lip will drawl the last dissent,
Some Union-saving patriot of your own
Lament to find his occupation gone.
'Grant that the North's insulted, scorned, betrayed,
O'erreached in bargains with her neighbor made,
When selfish thrift and party held the scales
For peddling dicker, not for honest sales,
Whom shall we strike? Who most deserves our blame?
The braggart Southron, open in his aim,
And bold as wicked, crashing straight through all
That bars his purpose, like a cannon-ball?
Or the mean traitor, breathing northern air,
With nasal speech and puritanic hair,
Whose cant the loss of principle survives,
As the mud-turtle e'en its head outlives;
Who, caught, chin-buried in some foul offence,
Puts on a look of injured innocence,
And consecrates his baseness to the cause
Of constitution, union, and the laws?

'Praise to the place-man who can hold aloof
His still unpurchased manhood, office-proof;
Who on his round of duty walks erect,
And leaves it only rich in self-respect;
As More maintained his virtue's lofty port
In the Eighth Henry's base and bloody court.
But, if exceptions here and there are found,
Who tread thus safely on enchanted ground,
The normal type, the fitting symbol still
Of those who fatten at the public mill,
Is the chained dog beside his master's door,
Or Circe's victim, feeding on all four!
'Give me the heroes who, at tuck of drum,
Salute thy staff, immortal Quattlebum!
Or they who, doubly armed with vote and gun,
Following thy lead, illustrious Atchison,
Their drunken franchise shift from scene to scene,
As tile-beard Jourdan did his guillotine!
Rather than him who, born beneath our skies,
To Slavery's hand its supplest tool supplies;
The party felon whose unblushing face
Looks from the pillory of his bribe of place,
And coolly makes a merit of disgrace,
Points to the footmarks of indignant scorn,
Shows the deep scars of satire's tossing horn;
And passes to his credit side the sum
Of all that makes a scoundrel's martyrdom!
' Bane of the North, its canker and its moth!
These modern Esaus, bartering rights for broth!
Taxing our justice, with their double claim,
As fools for pity, and as knaves for blame;
Who, urged by party, sect, or trade, within
The fell embrace of Slavery's sphere of sin,
Part at the outset with their moral sense,
The watchful angel set for Truth's defence;
Confound all contrasts, good and ill; reverse
The poles of life, its blessing and its curse;
And lose thenceforth from their perverted sight
The eternal difference 'twixt the wrong and right;
To them the Law is but the iron span
That girds the ankles of imbruted man;
To them the Gospel has no higher aim
Than simple sanction of the master's claim,
Dragged in the slime of Slavery's loathsome trail,
Like Chalier's Bible at his ass's tail!
'Such are the men who, with instinctive dread,
Whenever Freedom lifts her drooping head,
Make prophet-tripods of their office-stools,
And scare the nurseries and the village schools
With dire presage of ruin grim and great,
A broken Union and a foundered State!
Such are the patriots, self-bound to the stake

Of office, martyrs for their country's sake:
Who fill themselves the hungry jaws of Fate,
And by their loss of manhood save the State.
In the wide gulf themselves like Curtius throw,
And test the virtues of cohesive dough;
As tropic monkeys, linking heads and tails,
Bridge o'er some torrent of Ecuador's vales!
'Such are the men who in your churches rave
To swearing-point, at mention of the slave!
When some poor parsons haply unawares,
Stammers of freedom in his timid prayers;
Who, if some foot-sore negro through the town
Steals northward, volunteer to hunt him down.
Or, if some neighbor, flying from disease,
Courts the mild balsam of the Southern breeze,
With hue and cry pursue him on his track,
And write Free-soiler on the poor man's back.
Such are the men who leave the pedler's cart,
While faring South, to learn the driver's art,
Or, in white neckcloth, soothe with pious aim
The graceful sorrows of some languid dame,
Who, from the wreck of her bereavement, saves
The double charm of widowhood and slaves!
Pliant and apt, they lose no chance to show
To what base depths apostasy can go;
Outdo the natives in their readiness
To roast a negro, or to mob a press;
Poise a tarred schoolmate on the lyncher's rail,
Or make a bonfire of their birthplace mail!
'So some poor wretch, whose lips no longer bear
The sacred burden of his mother's prayer,
By fear impelled, or lust of gold enticed,
Turns to the Crescent from the Cross of Christ,
And, over-acting in superfluous zeal,
Crawls prostrate where the faithful only kneel,
Out-howls the Dervish, hugs his rags to court
The squalid Santon's sanctity of dirt;
And, when beneath the city gateway's span
Files slow and long the Meccan caravan,
And through its midst, pursued by Islam's prayers,
The prophet's Word some favored camel bears,
The marked apostate has his place assigned
The Koran-bearer's sacred rump behind,
With brush and pitcher following, grave and mute,
In meek attendance on the holy brute!
' Men of the North! beneath your very eyes,
By hearth and home, your real danger lies.
Still day by day some hold of freedom falls
Through home-bred traitors fed within its walls.
Men whom yourselves with vote and purse sustain,
At posts of honor, influence, and gain;
The right of Slavery to your sons to teach,

And 'South-side' Gospels in your pulpits preach,
Transfix the Law to ancient freedom dear
On the sharp point of her subverted spear,
And imitate upon her cushion plump
The mad Missourian lynching from his stump;
Or, in your name, upon the Senate's floor
Yield up to Slavery all it asks, and more;
And, ere your dull eyes open to the cheat,
Sell your old homestead underneath your feet!
While such as these your loftiest outlooks hold,
While truth and conscience with your wares are sold,
While grave-browed merchants band themselves to aid
An annual man-hunt for their Southern trade,
What moral power within your grasp remains
To stay the mischief on Nebraska's plains?
High as the tides of generous impulse flow,
As far rolls back the selfish undertow;
And all your brave resolves, though aimed as true
As the horse-pistol Balmawhapple drew,
To Slavery's bastions lend as slight a shock
As the poor trooper's shot to Stirling rock!
'Yet, while the need of Freedom's cause demands
The earnest efforts of your hearts and hands,
Urged by all motives that can prompt the heart
To prayer and toil and manhood's manliest part;
Though to the soul's deep tocsin Nature joins
The warning whisper of her Orphic pines,
The north-wind's anger, and the south-wind's sigh,
The midnight sword-dance of the northern sky,
And, to the ear that bends above the sod
Of the green grave-mounds.in the Fields of God,
In low, deep murmurs of rebuke or cheer,
The land's dead fathers speak their hope or fear,
Yet let not Passion wrest from Reason's hand
The guiding rein and symbol of command.
Blame not the caution proffering to your zeal
A well-meant drag upon its hurrying wheel;
Nor chide the man whose honest doubt extends
To the means only, not the righteous ends;
Nor fail to weigh the scruples and the fears
Of milder natures and serener years.
In the long strife with evil which began
With the first lapse of new-created man,
Wisely and well has Providence assigned
To each his part, some forward, some behind;
And they, too, serve who temper and restrain
The o'erwarm heart that sets on fire the brain.
True to yourselves, feed Freedom's altar-flame
With what you have; let others do the same.
Spare timid doubters; set like flint your face
Against the self-sold knaves of gain and place:
Pity the weak; but with unsparing hand

Cast out the traitors who infest the land;
From bar, press, pulpit, east them everywhere,
By dint of fasting, if you fail by prayer.
And in their place bring men of antique mould,
Like the grave fathers of your Age of Gold;
Statesmen like those who sought the primal fount
Of righteous law, the Sermon on the Mount;
Lawyers who prize, like Quincy, (to our day
Still spared, Heaven bless him!) honor more than pay,
And Christian jurists, starry-pure, like Jay;
Preachers like Woolman, or like them who bore
The faith of Wesley to our Western shore,
And held no convert genuine till he broke
Alike his servants' and the Devil's yoke;
And priests like him who Newport's market trod,
And o'er its slave-ships shook the bolts of God!
So shall your power, with a wise prudence used,
Strong but forbearing, firm but not abused,
In kindly keeping with the good of all,
The nobler maxims of the past recall,
Her natural home-born right to Freedom give,
And leave her foe his robber-right, to live.
Live, as the snake does in his noisome fen!
Live, as the wolf does in his bone-strewn den!
Live, clothed with cursing like a robe of flame,
The focal point of million-fingered shame!
Live, till the Southron, who, with all his faults,
Has manly instincts, in his pride revolts,
Dashes from off him, midst the glad world's cheers,
The hideous nightmare of his dream of years,
And lifts, self-prompted, with his own right hand,
The vile encumbrance from his glorious land!
'So, wheresoe'er our destiny sends forth
Its widening circles to the South or North,
Where'er our banner flaunts beneath the stars
Its mimic splendors and its cloudlike bars,
There shall Free Labor's hardy children stand
The equal sovereigns of a slaveless land.
And when at last the hunted bison tires,
And dies o'ertaken by the squatter's fires;
And westward, wave on wave, the living flood
Breaks on the snow-line of majestic Hood;
And lonely Shasta listening hears the tread
Of Europe's fair-haired children, Hesper-led;
And, gazing downward through his hoar-locks, sees
The tawny Asian climb his giant knees,
The Eastern sea shall hush his waves to hear
Pacific's surf-beat answer Freedom's cheer,
And one long rolling fire of triumph run
Between the sunrise and the sunset gun!'
My task is done. The Showman and his show,
Themselves but shadows, Into shadows go;

And, if no song of idlesse I have sung,
Nor tints of beauty on the canvas flung;
If the harsh numbers grate on tender ears,
And the rough picture overwrought appears;
With deeper coloring, with a sterner blast,
Before my soul a voice and vision passed,
Such as might Milton's jarring trump require,
Or glooms of Dante fringed with lurid fire.
Oh; not of choice, for themes of public wrong
I leave the green and pleasant paths of song,
The mild, sweet words which soften and adorn,
For sharp rebuke and bitter laugh of scorn.
More dear to me some song of private worth,
Some homely idyl of my native North,
Some summer pastoral of her inland vales,
Or, grim and weird, her winter fireside tales
Haunted by ghosts of unreturning sails;
Lost barks at parting hung from stem to helm
With prayers of love like dreams on Virgil's elm.
Nor private grief nor malice holds my pen;
I owe but kindness to my fellow-men;
And, South or North, wherever hearts of prayer
Their woes and weakness to our Father bear,
Wherever fruits of Christian love are found
In holy lives, to me is holy ground.
But the time passes. It were vain to crave
A late indulgence. What I had I gave.
Forget the poet, but his warning heed,
And shame his poor word with your nobler deed.

Anniversary Poem
Once, more, dear friends, you meet beneath
A clouded sky:
Not yet the sword has found its sheath,
And on the sweet spring airs the breath
Of war floats by.
Yet trouble springs not from the ground,
Nor pain from chance;
The Eternal order circles round,
And wave and storm find mete and bound
In Providence.
Full long our feet the flowery ways
Of peace have trod,
Content with creed and garb and phrase:
A harder path in earlier days
Led up to God.
Too cheaply truths, once purchased dear,
Are made our own;
Too long the world has smiled to hear
Our boast of full corn in the ear
By others sown;

To see us stir the martyr fires
Of long ago,
And wrap our satisfied desires
In the singed mantles that our sires
Have dropped below.
But now the cross our worthies bore
On us is laid;
Profession's quiet sleep is o'er,
And in the scale of truth once more
Our faith is weighed.
The cry of innocent blood at last
Is calling down
An answer in the whirlwind-blast,
The thunder and the shadow cast
From Heaven's dark frown.
The land is red with judgments. Who
Stands guiltless forth?
Have we been faithful as we knew,
To God and to our brother true,
To Heaven and Earth?
How faint, through din of merchandise
And count of gain,
Have seemed to us the captive's cries!
How far away the tears and sighs
Of souls in pain!
This day the fearful reckoning comes
To each and all;
We hear amidst our peaceful homes
The summons of the conscript drums,
The bugle's call.
Our path is plain; the war-net draws
Round us in vain,
While, faithful to the Higher Cause,
We keep our fealty to the laws
Through patient pain.
The levelled gun, the battle-brand,
We may not take:
But, calmly loyal, we can stand
And suffer with our suffering land
For conscience' sake.
Why ask for ease where all is pain?
Shall we alone
Be left to add our gain to gain,
When over Armageddon's plain
The trump is blown?
To suffer well is well to serve;
Safe in our Lord
The rigid lines of law shall curve
To spare us; from our heads shall swerve
Its smiting sword.
And light is mingled with the gloom,
And joy with grief;

Divinest compensations come,
Through thorns of judgment mercies bloom
In sweet relief.
Thanks for our privilege to bless,
By word and deed,
The widow in her keen distress,
The childless and the fatherless,
The hearts that bleed!
For fields of duty, opening wide,
Where all our powers
Are tasked the eager steps to guide
Of millions on a path untried:
The slave is ours!
Ours by traditions dear and old,
Which make the race
Our wards to cherish and uphold,
And cast their freedom in the mould
Of Christian grace.
And we may tread the sick-bed floors
Where strong men pine,
And, down the groaning corridors,
Pour freely from our liberal stores
The oil and wine.
Who murmurs that in these dark days
His lot is cast?
God's hand within the shadow lays
The stones whereon His gates of praise
Shall rise at last.
Turn and o'erturn, O outstretched Hand!
Nor stint, nor stay;
The years have never dropped their sand
On mortal issue vast and grand
As ours to-day.
Already, on the sable ground
Of man's despair
Is Freedom's glorious picture found,
With all its dusky hands unbound
Upraised in prayer.
Oh, small shall seem all sacrifice
And pain and loss,
When God shall wipe the weeping eyes,
For suffering give the victor's prize,
The crown for cross!

Astræa At The Capitol
When first I saw our banner wave
Above the nation's council-hall,
I heard beneath its marble wall
The clanking fetters of the slave!

In the foul market-place I stood,

And saw the Christian mother sold,
And childhood with its locks of gold,
Blue-eyed and fair with Saxon blood.

I shut my eyes, I held my breath,
And, smothering down the wrath and shame
That set my Northern blood aflame,
Stood silent, where to speak was death.

Beside me gloomed the prison-cell
Where wasted one in slow decline
For uttering simple words of mine,
And loving freedom all too well.

The flag that floated from the dome
Flapped menace in the morning air;
I stood a perilled stranger where
The human broker made his home.

For crime was virtue: Gown and Sword
And Law their threefold sanction gave,
And to the quarry of the slave
Went hawking with our symbol-bird.

On the oppressor's side was power;
And yet I knew that every wrong,
However old, however strong,
But waited God's avenging hour.

I knew that truth would crush the lie,
Somehow, some time, the end would be;
Yet scarcely dared I hope to see
The triumph with my mortal eye.

But now I see it! In the sun
A free flag floats from yonder dome,
And at the nation's hearth and home
The justice long delayed is done.

Not as we hoped, in calm of prayer,
The message of deliverance comes,
But heralded by roll of drums
On waves of battle-troubled air!

Midst sounds that madden and appall,
The song that Bethlehem's shepherds knew!
The harp of David melting through
The demon-agonies of Saul!

Not as we hoped; but what are we?
Above our broken dreams and plans
God lays, with wiser hand than man's,

The corner-stones of liberty.

I cavil not with Him: the voice
That freedom's blessed gospel tells
Is sweet to me as silver bells,
Rejoicing! yea, I will rejoice!

Dear friends still toiling in the sun;
Ye dearer ones who, gone before,
Are watching from the eternal shore
The slow work by your hands begun,

Rejoice with me! The chastening rod
Blossoms with love; the furnace heat
Grows cool beneath His blessed feet
Whose form is as the Son of God!

Rejoice! Our Marah's bitter springs
Are sweetened; on our ground of grief
Rise day by day in strong relief
The prophecies of better things.

Rejoice in hope! The day and night
Are one with God, and one with them
Who see by faith the cloudy hem
Of Judgement fringed with Mercy's light

At Washington

With a cold and wintry noon-light.
On its roofs and steeples shed,
Shadows weaving with t e sunlight
From the gray sky overhead,
Broadly, vaguely, all around me, lies the half-built town outspread.
Through this broad street, restless ever,
Ebbs and flows a human tide,
Wave on wave a living river;
Wealth and fashion side by side;
Toiler, idler, slave and master, in the same quick current glide.
Underneath yon dome, whose coping
Springs above them, vast and tall,
Grave men in the dust are groping.
For the largess, base and small,
Which the hand of Power is scattering, crumbs which from its table fall.
Base of heart! They vilely barter
Honor's wealth for party's place;
Step by step on Freedom's charter
Leaving footprints of disgrace;
For to-day's poor pittance turning from the great hope of their race.
Yet, where festal lamps are throwing
Glory round the dancer's hair,
Gold-tressed, like an angel's, flowing

Backward on the sunset air;
And the low quick pulse of music beats its measure sweet and rare:
There to-night shall woman's glances,
Star-like, welcome give to them;
Fawning fools with shy advances
Seek to touch their garments' hem,
With the tongue of flattery glozing deeds which God and Truth condemn.
From this glittering lie my vision
Takes a broader, sadder range,
Full before me have arisen
Other pictures dark and strange;
From the parlor to the prison must the scene and witness change.
Hark! the heavy gate is swinging
On its hinges, harsh and slow;
One pale prison lamp is flinging
On a fearful group below
Such a light as leaves to terror whatsoe'er it does not show.
Pitying God! Is that a woman
On whose wrist the shackles clash?
Is that shriek she utters human,
Underneath the stinging lash?
Are they men whose eyes of madness from that sad procession flash?
Still the dance goes gayly onward!
What is it to Wealth and Pride
That without the stars are looking
On a scene which earth should hide?
That the slave-ship lies in waiting, rocking on Potomac's tide!
Vainly to that mean Ambition
Which, upon a rival's fall,
Winds above its old condition,
With a reptile's slimy crawl,
Shall the pleading voice of sorrow, shall the slave in anguish call.
Vainly to the child of Fashion,
Giving to ideal woe
Graceful luxury of compassion,
Shall the stricken mourner go;
Hateful seems the earnest sorrow, beautiful the hollow show!
Nay, my words are all too sweeping:
In this crowded human mart,
Feeling is not dead, but sleeping;
Man's strong will and woman's heart,
In the coming strife for Freedom, yet shall bear their generous part.
And from yonder sunny valleys,
Southward in the distance lost,
Freedom yet shall summon allies
Worthier than the North can boast,
With the Evil by their hearth-stones grappling at severer cost.
Now, the soul alone is willing.
Faint the heart and weak the knee;
And as yet no lip is thrilling
With the mighty words, 'Be Free!'
Tarrieth long the land's Good Angel, but his advent is to be!

Meanwhile, turning from the revel
To the prison-cell my sight,
For intenser hate of evil,
For a keener sense of right,
Shaking off thy dust, I thank thee, City of the Slaves, to-night!
'To thy duty now and ever!
Dream no more of rest or stay:
Give to Freedom's great endeavor
All thou art and hast to-day:'
Thus, above the city's murmur, saith a Voice, or seems to say.
Ye with heart and vision gifted
To discern and love the right,
Whose worn faces have been lifted
To the slowly-growing light,
Where from Freedom's sunrise drifted slowly back the murk of night!
Ye who through long years of trial
Still have held your purpose fast,
While a lengthening shade the dial
From the westering sunshine cast,
And of hope each hour's denial seemed an echo of the last!
O my brothers! O my sisters!
Would to God that ye were near,
Gazing with me down the vistas
Of a sorrow strange and drear;
Would to God that ye were listeners to the Voice I seem to hear!
With the storm above us driving,
With the false earth mined below,
Who shall marvel if thus striving
We have counted friend as foe;
Unto one another giving in the darkness blow for blow.
Well it may be that our natures
Have grown sterner and more hard,
And the freshness of their features
Somewhat harsh and battle-scarred,
And their harmonies of feeling overtasked and rudely jarred.
Be it so. It should not swerve us
From a purpose true and brave;
Dearer Freedom's rugged service
Than the pastime of the slave;
Better is the storm above it than the quiet of the grave.
Let us then, uniting, bury
All our idle feuds in dust,
And to future conflicts carry
Mutual faith and common trust;
Always he who most forgiveth in his brother is most just.
From the eternal shadow rounding
All our sun and starlight here,
Voices of our lost ones sounding
Bid us be of heart and cheer,
Through the silence, down the spaces, falling on the inward ear.
Know we not our dead are looking
Downward with a sad surprise,

All our strife of words rebuking
With their mild and loving eyes?
Shall we grieve the holy angels? Shall we cloud their blessed skies?
Let us draw their mantles o'er us,
Which have fallen in our way;
Let us do the work before us,
Cheerly, bravely, while we may,
Ere the long night-silence cometh, and with us it is not day!

Brown Of Ossawatomie

John Brown of Ossawatomie spake on his dying day:
'I will not have to shrive my soul a priest in Slavery's pay.
But let some poor slave-mother whom I have striven to free,
With her children, from the gallows-stair put up a prayer for me!'

John Brown of Ossawatomie, they led him out to die;
And lo! a poor slave-mother with her little child pressed nigh.
Then the bold, blue eye grew tender, and the old harsh face grew mild,
As he stooped between the jeering ranks and kissed the negro's child.

The shadows of his stormy life that moment fell apart;
And they who blamed the bloody hand forgave the loving heart.
That kiss from all its guilty means redeemed the good intent,
And round the grisly fighter's hair the martyr's aureole bent!

Perish with him the folly that seeks through evil good
Long live the generous purpose unstained with human blood!
Not the raid of midnight terror, but the thought which underlies;
Not the borderer's pride of daring, but the Christian's sacrifice.

Nevermore may yon Blue Ridges the Northern rifle hear,
Nor see the light of blazing homes flash on the negro's spear.
But let the free-winged angel Truth their guarded passes scale,
To teach that right is more than might, and justice more than mail!

So vainly shall Virginia set her battle in array;
In vain her trampling squadrons knead the winter snow with clay.
She may strike the pouncing eagle, but she dares not harm the dove;
And every gate she bars to Hate shall open wide to Love!

Burial Of Barber

Bear him, comrades, to his grave;
Never over one more brave
Shall the prairie grasses weep,
In the ages yet to come,
When the millions in our room,
What we sow in tears, shall reap.
Bear him up the icy hill,
With the Kansas, frozen still
As his noble heart, below,

And the land he came to till
With a freeman's thews and will,
And his poor hut roofed with snow!

One more look of that dead face,
Of his murder's ghastly trace!
One more kiss, O widowed one!
Lay your left hands on his brow,
Lift you right hands up and vow
That his work shall yet be done.

Patience, friends! The eye of God
Every path by Murder trod
Watches, lidless, day and night;
And the dead man in his shroud,
And his widow weeping loud,
And our hearts, are in his sight.

Every deadly threat that swells
With the roar of gambling hells,
Every brutal jest and jeer,
Every wicked thought and plan
Of the cruel heart of man,
Though but whispered, He can hear!

We in suffering, they in crime,
Wait the just award of time,
Wait the vengeance that is due;
Not in vain a heart shall break,
Not a tear for Freedom's sake
Fall unheeded: God is true.

While the flag with stars bedecked
Threatens where it should protect,
And the Law shakes hands with Crime,
What is left us but to wait,
Match our patience to our fate,
And abide the better time?

Patience, friends! The human heart
Everywhere shall take our part,
Everywhere for us shall pray;
On our side are nature's laws,
And God's life is in the cause
That we suffer for to-day.

Well to suffer is divine;
Pass the watchword down the line,
Pass the countersign: 'Endure.'
Not to him who rashly dares,
But to him who nobly bears,
Is the victor's garland sure.

Frozen earth to frozen breast,
Lay our slain one down to rest;
Lay him down in hope and faith,
And above the broken sod,
Once again, to Freedom's God,
Pledge ourselves for life or death,

That the State whose walls we lay,
In our blood and tears, to-day,
Shall be free from bonds of shame,
And our goodly land untrod
By the feet of Slavery, shod
With cursing as with flame!

Plant the Buckeye on his grave,
For the hunter of the slave
In its shadow cannot rest;
And let martyr mound and tree
Be our pledge and guaranty
Of the freedom of the West!

Burning Drift-Wood

Before my drift-wood fire I sit,
And see, with every waif I burn,
Old dreams and fancies coloring it,
And folly's unlaid ghosts return.

O ships of mine, whose swift keels cleft
The enchanted sea on which they sailed,
Are these poor fragments only left
Of vain desires and hopes that failed?

Did I not watch from them the light
Of sunset on my towers in Spain,
And see, far off, uploom in sight
The Fortunate Isles I might not gain?

Did sudden lift of fog reveal
Arcadia's vales of song and spring,
And did I pass, with grazing keel,
The rocks whereon the sirens sing?

Have I not drifted hard upon
The unmapped regions lost to man,
The cloud-pitched tents of Prester John,
The palace domes of Kubla Khan?

Did land winds blow from jasmine flowers,
Where Youth the ageless Fountain fills?
Did Love make sign from rose blown bowers,

And gold from Eldorado's hills?

Alas! the gallant ships, that sailed
On blind Adventure's errand sent,
Howe'er they laid their courses, failed
To reach the haven of Content.

And of my ventures, those alone
Which Love had freighted, safely sped,
Seeking a good beyond my own,
By clear-eyed Duty piloted.

O mariners, hoping still to meet
The luck Arabian voyagers met,
And find in Bagdad's moonlit street,
Haroun al Raschid walking yet,

Take with you, on your Sea of Dreams,
The fair, fond fancies dear to youth.
I turn from all that only seems,
And seek the sober grounds of truth.

What matter that it is not May,
That birds have flown, and trees are bare,
That darker grows the shortening day,
And colder blows the wintry air!

The wrecks of passion and desire,
The castles I no more rebuild,
May fitly feed my drift-wood fire,
And warm the hands that age has chilled.

Whatever perished with my ships,
I only know the best remains;
A song of praise is on my lips
For losses which are now my gains.

Heap high my hearth! No worth is lost;
No wisdom with the folly dies.
Burn on, poor shreds, your holocaust
Shall be my evening sacrifice!

Far more than all I dared to dream,
Unsought before my door I see;
On wings of fire and steeds of steam
The world's great wonders come to me,

And holier signs, unmarked before,
Of Love to seek and Power to save,
The righting of the wronged and poor,
The man evolving from the slave;

And life, no longer chance or fate,
Safe in the gracious Fatherhood.
I fold o'er-wearied hands and wait,
In full assurance of the good.

And well the waiting time must be,
Though brief or long its granted days,
If Faith and Hope and Charity
Sit by my evening hearth-fire's blaze.

And with them, friends whom Heaven has spared,
Whose love my heart has comforted,
And, sharing all my joys, has shared
My tender memories of the dead,

Dear souls who left us lonely here,
Bound on their last, long voyage, to whom
We, day by day, are drawing near,
Where every bark has sailing room.

I know the solemn monotone
Of waters calling unto me;
I know from whence the airs have blown
That whisper of the Eternal Sea.

As low my fires of drift-wood burn,
I hear that sea's deep sounds increase,
And, fair in sunset light, discern
Its mirage-lifted Isles of Peace.

Cassandra Southwick

To the God of all sure mercies let my blessing rise today,
From the scoffer and the cruel He hath plucked the spoil away;
Yes, he who cooled the furnace around the faithful three,
And tamed the Chaldean lions, hath set His handmaid free!

Last night I saw the sunset melt though my prison bars,
Last night across my damp earth-floor fell the pale gleam of stars;
In the coldness and the darkness all through the long night-time,
My grated casement whitened with autumn's early rime.

Alone, in that dark sorrow, hour after hour crept by;
Star after star looked palely in and sank adown the sky;
No sound amid night's stillness, save that which seemed to be
The dull and heavy beating of the pulses of the sea;

All night I sat unsleeping, for I knew that on the morrow
The ruler said the cruel priest would mock me in my sorrow,
Dragged to their place of market, and bargained for and sold,
Like a lamb before the shambles, like a heifer from the fold!

Oh, the weakness of the flesh was there‾the shrinking and the shame;
And the low voice of the Tempter like whispers to me came,
'Why sit'st thou thus forlornly,' the wicked murmur said,
'Damp walls thy bower beauty, cold earth thy maiden bed?

'Where be the smiling faces, and voices soft and sweet,
Seen in thy father's dwelling, hoard in the pleasant street?
Where be the youths whose glances, the summer Sabbath through,
Turned tenderly and timidly unto thy father's pew?

'Why sit'st thou here, Cassandra? Bethink thee with what mirth
Thy happy schoolmates gather around the warm, dark hearth;
How the crimson shadows tremble on foreheads white and fair,
On eyes of merry girlhood, half hid in golden hair.

'Not for thee the hearth-fire brightens, not for thee kind words are spoken,
Not for thee the nuts of Wenham woods by laughing boys are broken;
No first-fruits of the orchard within thy lap are laid,
For thee no flowers of autumn the youthful hunters braid.

'O weak, deluded maiden!‾by crazy fancies led,
With wild and raving railers an evil path to tread;
To leave a wholesome worship, and teaching pure and sound,
And mate with maniac women, loose-haired and sackcloth-bound,

'And scoffers of the priesthood, who mock at things divine,
Who rail against thy pulpit, and holy bread and wine;
Bore from their cart-tail scourgings, and from the pillory lame,
Rejoicing in their wretchedness, and glorying in their shame.

'And what a fate awaits thee! a sadly toiling slave,
Dragging the slowly lengthening chain of bondage to the grave!
Think of thy woman's nature, subdued in hopeless thrall,
The easy prey of any, the scoff and scorn of all!'

Oh, ever as the Tempter spoke, and feecle Nature's fears
Wrung drop by drop the scalding flow of unavailing tears,
I wrestled down the evil thoughts, and strove in silent prayer
To feel, O Helper of the weak! that Thou indeed wert there!

I thought of Paul and Silas, within Philippi's call,
And how from Peter's sleeping limbs the prison shackles fell,
Till I seemed to hear the trailing of an Angel's robe of white,
And to feel a blessed presence invisible to sight.

Bless the Lord for all his mercies! for the peace and love I felt,
Like the dew of Hermon's holy hill, upon my spirit melt;
When 'Get behind me, Satan! ' was the language of my heart,
And I felt the Evil Tempter with all his doubts depart.

Slow broke the gray cold morning; again the sunshine fell,
Flocked with the shade of bar and grate within my lonely cell;

The hoar-frost melted on the wall, and upward from the street
Came careless laugh and idle word, and tread of passing feet.

At length the heavy bolts fell back, my door was open cast,
And slowly at the sheriff's side, up the long street I passed;
I heard the murmur round me, and felt, but dared not see,
How, from every door and window, the people gazed on me.

And doubt and fear fell on me, shame burned upon my cheek,
Swam earth and sky around me, my trembling limbs grew weak;
'Oh Lord, support thy handmaid, and from her soul cast out
The fear of men, which brings a snare, the weakness and the doubt.

Then the dreary shadows scattered, like a cloud in morning's breeze,
And a low deep voice within me seemed whispering words like these:
'Though thy earth be as the iron, and thy heaven a brazen wall,
Trust still His loving-kindness whose power is over all.'

We paused at length, where at my feet the sunlit waters broke
On glaring roach of shining beach, and shingly wall of rock;
The merchant-ships lay idle there, in hard clear lines on high,
Treeing with rope and slender spar their network on the sky.

And there were ancient citizens, cloak-wrapped and grave and cold,
And grim and stout sea-captains with faces bronzed and old,
And on his horse, with Rawson, his cruel clerk at hand,
Sat dark and haughty Endicott, the ruler of the land.

And poisoning with his evil words the ruler's ready ear,
The priest leaned over his saddle, with laugh and scoff and jeer;
It stirred my soul, and from my lips the soul of silence broke,
As if through woman's weakness a warning spirit spoke.

I cried 'The Lord rebuke thee, thou smiter of the meek,
Thou robber of the righteous, thou trampler of the weak!
Go light the cold, dark hearth-stones, go turn the prison lock
Of the poor hearts though hast hunted, thou wolf amid the flock!'

Dark lowered the brows of Endicott, and with a deeper red
O'er Rawson's wine-empurpled cheek the flash of anger spread;
'Good people, ' quoth the white-lipped priest, 'heed not her words so wild,
Her Master speaks within her the Devil owns his child!'

But gray heads shook, and young brows knit, the while the sheriff read
That law the wicked rulers against the poor have made,
Who to their house of Rimmon and idol priesthood bring
No bonded knee of worship, nor gainful offering.

Then to the stout sea-captains the sheriff, turning, said
'Wish of ye, worthy seamen, will take this Quaker maid?
On the Isle of fair Barbados, or on Virginia's shore
You may hold her at a higher price than Indian girl or Moor!'

Grim and silent stood the captains; and when again he cried,
'Speak out my worthy seamen!' no voice, no sign replied;
But I felt a hard hand press my own, and kind words met my ear,
'God bless thee, and preserve thee, my gentle girl and dear!'

A weight seemed lifted from my heart, a pitying friend was nigh,
I felt it in his hard, rough hand, and saw it in his eye;
And when again the sheriff spoke, that voice, so kind to me,
Growled back its stormy answer like the roaring of the sea.

'Pile my ship with bars of silver, pack with coins of Spanish gold
From keel-piece up to deck-plank, the roomage of her hold,
By the living God that made me! I would sooner in your bay
Sink ship and crew and cargo, than bear this child away!'

'Well answered, worthy captain, shame on their cruel laws!'
Ran through the crowd in murmurs loud the people's just applause.
'Like the herdsmen of Tekoa, In Israel of old,
Shall we see the poor and righteous again for silver sold?'

I looked on haughty Endicott; with weapon half-way drawn,
Swept around the throng his lion glare of bitter hate and scorn;
Fiercely he drew his bridle-rain, and turned in silence back,
And sneering priest and baffled clerk rode murmuring in his track.

Hard after them the sheriff looked, in bitterness of soul,
Thrice smote his staff upon the ground, and crushed his parchment-roll.
'Good friends,' he said, 'since both have fled, the ruler and the priest
Judge ye, if from their further work I be not well released.'

Loud was the cheer which, full and clear, swept round the silent bay,
As, with kind words and kinder looks, he bade me go my way;
For he who turns the courses of the streamlet of the glen,
And the river of great waters, had turned the hearts of men.

Oh, at that hour the very earth seemed changed beneath my eye,
A holier wonder round no rose the blue walls of the sky,
A lovelier light on rock and hill and stream and woodland lay,
And softer lapsed on sunnier sands the waters of the bay.

Thanksgiving to the Lord of life! To him all praises be,
Who from the hands of evil men hath set his handmaid free;
All praise to Him before whose power the mighty are afraid,
Who take the crafty in the snare which for the poor is laid!

Sing, O my soul, rejoicingly, on evening's twilight calm
Uplift the loud thanksgiving, pour forth the grateful psalm;
Let all dear hearts with me rejoice, as did the saints of old,
When of the Lord's good angel the rescued Peter told.

And weep and howl, ye evil priests and mighty men of wrong,

The lord shall smite the proud, and lay His hand upon the strong.
Woe to the wicked rulers in his avenging hour!
Woe to the wolves who seek the flocks to raven and devour!

But let the humble ones arise, the poor in heart be glad,
And let the mourning ones again with robes of praise be clad,
For he who cooled the furnace, and smoothed the stormy wave,
And tamed the Chaldean lions, is mighty still to save!

Clerical Oppressors

Just God! and these are they
Who minister at thine altar, God of Right!
Men who their hands with prayer and blessing lay
On Israel's Ark of light!
What! preach, and kidnap men?
Give thanks, and rob thy own afflicted poor?
Talk of thy glorious liberty, and then
Bolt hard the captive's door?
What! servants of thy own
Merciful Son, who came to seek and save
The homeless and the outcast, fettering down
The tasked and plundered slave!
Pilate and Herod, friends!
Chief priests and rulers, as of old, combine!
Just God and holy! is that church, which lends
Strength to the spoiler, thine?
Paid hypocrites, who turn
Judgment aside, and rob the Holy Book
Of those high words of truth which search and burn
In warning and rebuke;
Feed fat, ye locusts, feed!
And, in your tasselled pulpits, thank the Lord
That, from the toiling bondman's utter need,
Ye pile your own full board.
How long, O Lord! how long
Shall such a priesthood barter truth away,
And in Thy name, for robbery and wrong
At Thy own altars pray?
Is not Thy hand stretched forth
Visibly in the heavens, to awe and smite?
Shall not the living God of all the earth,
And heaven above, do right?
Woe, then, to all who grind
Their brethren of a common Father down!
To all who plunder from the immortal mind
Its bright and glorious crown!
Woe to the priesthood! woe
To those whose hire is with the price of blood;
Perverting, darkening, changing, as they go,
The searching truths of God!
Their glory and their might.

Shall perish; and their very names shall be
Vile before all the people, in the light
Of a world's liberty.
Oh, speed the moment on
When Wrong shall cease, and Liberty and Love
And Truth and Right throughout the earth be known
As in their home above.

Daniel Neall

I.

Friend of the Slave, and yet the friend of all;
Lover of peace, yet ever foremost when
The need of battling Freedom called for men
To plant the banner on the outer wall;
Gentle and kindly, ever at distress
Melted to more than woman's tenderness,
Yet firm and steadfast, at his duty's post
Fronting the violence of a maddened host,
Like some-gray rock from which the waves are tossed!
Knowing his deeds of love, men questioned not
The faith of one whose walk and word were right;
Who tranquilly in Life's great task-field wrought,
And, side by side with evil, scarcely caught
A stain upon his pilgrim garb of white:
Prompt to redress another's wrong, his own
Leaving to Time and Truth and Penitence alone.

II.

Such was our friend. Formed on the good old plan,
A true and brave and downright honest man!
He blew no trumpet in the market-place,
Nor in the church with hypocritic face
Supplied with cant the lack of Christian grace;
Loathing pretence, he did with cheerful will
What others talked of while their hands were still;
And, while 'Lord, Lord!' the pious tyrants cried,
Who, in the poor, their Master crucified,
His daily prayer, far better understood.
In acts than words, was simply doing good.
So calm, so constant was his rectitude,
That by his loss alone we know its worth,
And feel how true a man has walked with us on earth.

Democracy

Bearer of Freedom's holy light,
Breaker of Slavery's chain and rod,
The foe of all which pains the sight,
Or wounds the generous ear of God!
Beautiful yet thy temples rise,
Though there profaning gifts are thrown;

And fires unkindled of the skies
Are glaring round thy altar-stone.
Still sacred, though thy name be breathed
By those whose hearts thy truth deride;
And garlands, plucked from thee, are wreathed
Around the haughty brows of Pride.
Oh, ideal of my boyhood's time!
The faith in which my father stood,
Even when the sons of Lust and Crime
Had stained thy peaceful courts with blood!
Still to those courts my footsteps turn,
For through the mists which darken there,
I see the flame of Freedom burn,
The Kebla of the patriot's prayer!
The generous feeling, pure and warm,
Which owns the right of all divine;
The pitying heart, the helping arm,
The prompt self-sacrifice, are thine.
Beneath thy broad, impartial eye,
How fade the lines of caste and birth!
How equal in their suffering lie
The groaning multides of earth!
Still to a stricken brother true,
Whatever clime hath nurtured him;
As stooped to heal the wounded Jew
The worshipper of Gerizim.
By misery unrepelled, unawed
By pomp or power, thou seest a Man
In prince or peasant, slave or lord,
Pale priest, or swarthy artisan.
Through all disguise, form, place, or name,
Beneath the flaunting robes of sin,
Through poverty and squalid shame,
Thou lookest on the man within.
On man, as man, retaining yet,
Howe'er debased, and soiled, and dim,
The crown upon his forehead set,
The immortal gift of God to him.
And there is reverence in thy look;
For that frail form which mortals wear
The Spirit of the Holiest took,
And veiled His perfect brightness there.
Not from the shallow babbling fount
Of vain philosophy thou art;
He who of old on Syria's Mount
Thrilled, warmed, by turns, the listener's heart,
In holy words which cannot die,
In thoughts which angels leaned to know,
Proclaimed thy message from on high,
Thy mission to a world of woe.
That voice's echo hath not died!
From the blue lake of Galilee,

And Tabor's lonely mountain-side,
It calls a struggling world to thee.
Thy name and watchword o'er this land
I hear in every breeze that stirs,
And round a thousand altars stand
Thy banded party worshippers.
Not to these altars of a day,
At party's call, my gift I bring;
But on thy olden shrine I lay
A freeman's dearest offering:
The voiceless utterance of his will,
His pledge to Freedom and to Truth,
That manhood's heart remembers still
The homage of his generous youth.

Derne

Night on the city of the Moor!
On mosque and tomb, and white-walled shore,
On sea-waves, to whose ceaseless knock
The narrow harbor gates unlock,
On corsair's galley, carack tall,
And plundered Christian caraval!
The sounds of Moslem life are still;
No mule-bell tinkles down the hill;
Stretched in the broad court of the khan,
The dusty Bornou caravan
Lies heaped in slumber, beast and man;
The Sheik is dreaming in his tent,
His noisy Arab tongue o'erspent;
The kiosk's glimmering lights are gone,
The merchant with his wares withdrawn;
Rough pillowed on some pirate breast,
The dancing-girl has sunk to rest;
And, save where measured footsteps fall
Along the Bashaw's guarded wall,
Or where, like some bad dream, the Jew
Creeps stealthily his quarter through,
Or counts with fear his golden heaps,
The City of the Corsair sleeps!
But where yon prison long and low
Stands black against the pale star-glow,
Chafed by the ceaseless wash of waves,
There watch and pine the Christian slaves;
Rough-bearded men, whose far-off wives
Wear out with grief their lonely lives;
And youth, still flashing from his eyes
The clear blue of New England skies,
A treasured lock of whose soft hair
Now wakes some sorrowing mother's prayer;
Or, worn upon some maiden breast,
Stirs with the loving heart's unrest!

A bitter cup each life must drain,
The groaning earth is cursed with pain,
And, like the scroll the angel bore
The shuddering Hebrew seer before,
O'erwrit alike, without, within,
With all the woes which follow sin;
But, bitterest of the ills beneath
Whose load man totters down to death,
Is that which plucks the regal crown
Of Freedom from his forehead down,
And snatches from his powerless hand
The sceptred sign of self-command,
Effacing with the chain and rod
The image and the seal of God;
Till from his nature, day by day,
The manly virtues fall away,
And leave him naked, blind and mute,
The godlike merging in the brute!
Why mourn the quiet ones who die
Beneath affection's tender eye,
Unto their household and their kin
Like ripened corn-sheaves gathered in?
O weeper, from that tranquil sod,
That holy harvest-home of God,
Turn to the quick and suffering, shed
Thy tears upon the living dead!
Thank God above thy dear ones' graves,
They sleep with Him, they are not slaves.
What dark mass, down the mountain-sides
Swift-pouring, like a stream divides?
A long, loose, straggling caravan,
Camel and horse and arméd man.
The moon's low crescent, glimmering o'er
Its grave of waters to the shore,
Lights up that mountain cavalcade,
And gleams from gun and spear and blade
Near and more near! now o'er them falls
The shadow of the city walls.
Hark to the sentry's challenge, drowned
In the fierce trumpet's charging sound!
The rush of men, the musket's peal,
The short, sharp clang of meeting steel!
Vain, Moslem, vain thy lifeblood poured
So freely on thy foeman's sword!
Not to the swift nor to the strong
The battles of the right belong;
For he who strikes for Freedom wears
The armor of the captive's prayers,
And Nature proffers to his cause
The strength of her eternal laws;
While he whose arm essays to bind
And herd with common brutes his kind

Strives evermore at fearful odds
With Nature and the jealous gods,
And dares the dread recoil which late
Or soon their right shall vindicate.
'T is done, the hornëd crescent falls!
The star-flag flouts the broken walls!
Joy to the captive husband! joy
To thy sick heart, O brown-locked boy!
In sullen wrath the conquered Moor
Wide open flings your dungeon-door,
And leaves ye free from cell and chain,
The owners of yourselves again.
Dark as his allies desert-born,
Soiled with the battle's stain, and worn
With the long marches of his band
Through hottest wastes of rock and sand,
Scorched by the sun and furnace-breath
Of the red desert's wind of death,
With welcome words and grasping hands,
The victor and deliverer stands!
The tale is one of distant skies;
The dust of half a century lies
Upon it; yet its hero's name
Still lingers on the lips of Fame.
Men speak the praise of him who gave
Deliverance to the Moorman's slave,
Yet dare to brand with shame and crime
The heroes of our land and time,
The self-forgetful ones, who stake
Home, name, and life for Freedom's sake.
God mend his heart who cannot feel
The impulse of a holy zeal,
And sees not, with his sordid eyes,
The beauty of self-sacrifice!
Though in the sacred place he stands,
Uplifting consecrated hands,
Unworthy are his lips to tell
Of Jesus' martyr-miracle,
Or name aright that dread embrace
Of suffering for a fallen race!

Expostulation
Our fellow-countrymen in chains!
Slaves, in a land of light and law!
Slaves, crouching on the very plains
Where rolled the storm of Freedom's war!
A groan from Eutaw's haunted wood,
A. wail where Camden's martyrs fell,
By every shrine of patriot blood,
From Moultrie's wall and Jasper's well!

By storied hill and hallowed grot,
By mossy wood and marshy glen,
Whence rang of old the rifle-shot,
And hurrying shout of Marion's men!
The groan of breaking hearts is there,
The falling lash, the fetter's clank!
Slaves, slaves are breathing in that air
Which old De Kalb and Sumter drank!

What, ho! our countrymen in chains!
The whip on woman's shrinking flesh!
Our soil yet reddening with the stains
Caught from her scourging, warm and fresh!
What! mothers from their children riven!
What! God's own image bought and sold!
Americans to market driven,
And bartered as the brute for gold!

Speak! shall their agony of prayer
Come thrilling to our hearts in vain?
To us whose fathers scorned to bear
The paltry menace of a chain;
To us, whose boast is loud and long
Of holy Liberty and Light;
Say, shall these writhing slaves of Wrong
Plead vainly for their plundered Right?

What! shall we send, with lavish breath,
Our sympathies across the wave,
Where Manhood, on the field of death,
Strikes for his freedom or a grave?
Shall prayers go up, and hymns be sung
For Greece, the Moslem fetter spurning,
And millions hail with pen and tongue
Our light on all her altars burning?

Shall Belgium feel, and gallant France,
By Vendome's pile and Schoenbrun's wall,
And Poland, gasping on her lance,
The impulse of our cheering call?
And shall the slave, beneath our eye,
Clank o'er our fields his hateful chain?
And toss his fettered arms on high,
And groan for Freedom's gift, in vain?

Oh, say, shall Prussia's banner be
A refuge for the stricken slave?
And shall the Russian serf go free
By Baikal's lake and Neva's wave?
And shall the wintry-bosomed Dane
Relax the iron hand of pride,
And bid his bondmen cast the chain

From fettered soul and limb aside?

Shall every flap of England's flag
Proclaim that all around are free,
From farthest Ind to each blue crag
That beetles o'er the Western Sea?
And shall we scoff at Europe's kings,
When Freedom's fire is dim with us,
And round our country's altar clings
The damning shade of Slavery's curse?

Go, let us ask of Constantine
To loose his grasp on Poland's throat;
And beg the lord of Mahmoud's line
To spare the struggling Suliote;
Will not the scorching answer come
From turbaned Turk, and scornful Russ
'Go, loose your fettered slaves at home,
Then turn, and ask the like of us!'

Just God! and shall we calmly rest,
The Christian's scorn, the heathen's mirth,
Content to live the lingering jest
And by-word of a mocking Earth?
Shall our own glorious land retain
That curse which Europe scorns to bear?
Shall our own brethren drag the chain
Which not even Russia's menials wear?

Up, then, in Freedom's manly part,
From graybeard eld to fiery youth,
And on the nation's naked heart
Scatter the living coals of Truth!
Up! while ye slumber, deeper yet
The shadow of our fame is growing!
Up! while ye pause, our sun may set
In blood, around our altars flowing!

Oh! rouse ye, ere the storm comes forth,
The gathered wrath of God and man,
Like that which wasted Egypt's earth,
When hail and fire above it ran.
Hear ye no warnings in the air?
Feel ye no earthquake underneath?
Up, up! why will ye slumber where
The sleeper only wakes in death?

Rise now for Freedom! not in strife
Like that your sterner fathers saw,
The awful waste of human life,
The glory and the guilt of war:'
But break the chain, the yoke remove,

And smite to earth Oppression's rod,
With those mild arms of Truth and Love,
Made mighty through the living God!

Down let the shrine of Moloch sink,
And leave no traces where it stood;
Nor longer let its idol drink
His daily cup of human blood;
But rear another altar there,
To Truth and Love and Mercy given,
And Freedom's gift, and Freedom's prayer,
Shall call an answer down from Heaven!

Garrison

The storm and peril overpast,
The hounding hatred shamed and still,
Go, soul of freedom! take at last
The place which thou alone canst fill.
Confirm the lesson taught of old
Life saved for self is lost, while they
Who lose it in His service hold
The lease of God's eternal day.
Not for thyself, but for the slave
Thy words of thunder shook the world;
No selfish griefs or hatred gave
The strength wherewith thy bolts were hurled.
From lips that Sinai's trumpet blew
We heard a tender under song;
Thy very wrath from pity grew,
From love of man thy hate of wrong.
Now past and present are as one;
The life below is life above;
Thy mortal years have but begun
Thy immortality of love.
With somewhat of thy lofty faith
We lay thy outworn garment by,
Give death but what belongs to death,
And life the life that cannot die!
Not for a soul like thine the calm
Of selfish ease and joys of sense;
But duty, more than crown or palm,
Its own exceeding recompense.
Go up and on! thy day well done,
Its morning promise well fulfilled,
Arise to triumphs yet unwon,
To holier tasks that God has willed.
Go, leave behind thee all that mars
The work below of man for man;
With the white legions of the stars
Do service such as angels can.
Wherever wrong shall right deny

Or suffering spirits urge their plea,
Be thine a voice to smite the lie,
A hand to set the captive free!

How Mary Grew

With wisdom far beyond her years,
And graver than her wondering peers,
So strong, so mild, combining still
The tender heart and queenly will,
To conscience and to duty true,
So, up from childhood, Mary Grew!

Then in her gracious womanhood
She gave her days to doing good.
She dared the scornful laugh of men,
The hounding mob, the slanderer's pen.
She did the work she found to do,
A Christian heroine, Mary Grew!

The freed slave thanks her; blessing comes
To her from women's weary homes;
The wronged and erring find in her
Their censor mild and comforter.
The world were safe if but a few
Could grow in grace as Mary Grew!

So, New Year's Eve, I sit and say,
By this low wood-fire, ashen gray;
Just wishing, as the night shuts down,
That I could hear in Boston town,
In pleasant Chestnut Avenue,
From her own lips, how Mary Grew!

And hear her graceful hostess tell
The silver-voiced oracle
Who lately through her parlors spoke
As through Dodona's sacred oak,
A wiser truth than any told
By Sappho's lips of ruddy gold,
The way to make the world anew,
Is just to grow as Mary Grew

Howard At Atlanta

Right in the track where Sherman
Ploughed his red furrow,
Out of the narrow cabin,
Up from the cellar's burrow,
Gathered the little black people,
With freedom newly dowered,
Where, beside their Northern teacher,

Stood the soldier, Howard.
He listened and heard the children
Of the poor and long-enslavëd
Reading the words of Jesus,
Singing the songs of David.
Behold! the dumb lips speaking,
The blind eyes seeing!
Bones of the Prophet's vision
Warmed into being!
Transformed he saw them passing
Their new life's portal!
Almost it seemed the mortal
Put on the immortal.
No more with the beasts of burden,
No more with stone and clod,
But crowned with glory and honor
In the image of God!
There was the human chattel
Its manhood taking;
There, in each dark, brown statue,
A soul was waking!
The man of many battles,
With tears his eyelids pressing,
Stretched over those dusky foreheads
His one-armed blessing.
And he said: 'Who hears can never
Fear for or doubt you;
What shall I tell the children
Up North about you?'
Then ran round a whisper, a murmur,
Some answer devising;
And a little boy stood up: 'General,
Tell'em we're rising!'
O black boy of Atlanta!
But half was spoken:
The slave's chain and the master's
Alike are broken.
The one curse of the races
Held both in tether:
They are rising, all are rising,
The black and white together!
O brave men and fair women!
Ill comes of hate and scorning:
Shall the dark faces only
Be turned to morning?
Make Time your sole avenger,
All-healing, all-redressing;
Meet Fate half-way, and make it
A joy and blessing!

Not unto us who did but seek
The word that burned within to speak,
Not unto us this day belong
The triumph and exultant song.
Upon us fell in early youth
The burden of unwelcome truth,
And left us, weak and frail and few,
The censor's painful work to do.
Thenceforth our life a fight became,
The air we breathed was hot with blame;
For not with gauged and softened tone
We made the bondman's cause our own.
We bore, as Freedom's hope forlorn,
The private hate, the public scorn;
Yet held through all the paths we trod
Our faith in man and trust in God.
We prayed and hoped; but still, with awe,
The coming of the sword we saw;
We heard the nearing steps of doom,
We saw the shade of things to come.
In grief which they alone can feel
Who from a mother's wrong appeal,
With blended lines of fear and hope
We cast our country's horoscope.
For still within her house of life
We marked the lurid sign of strife,
And, poisoning and imbittering all,
We saw the star of Wormwood fall.
Deep as our love for her became
Our hate of all that wrought her shame,
And if, thereby, with tongue and pen
We erred, we were but mortal men.
We hoped for peace; our eyes survey
The blood-red dawn of Freedom's day:
We prayed for love to loose the chain;
'T is shorn by battle's axe in twain!
Nor skill nor strength nor zeal of ours
Has mined and heaved the hostile towers;
Not by our hands is turned the key
That sets the sighing captives free.
A redder sea than Egypt's wave
Is piled and parted for the slave;
A darker cloud moves on in light;
A fiercer fire is guide by night!
The praise, O Lord! is Thine alone,
In Thy own way Thy work is done!
Our poor gifts at Thy feet we cast,
To whom be glory, first and last!

Hymn For The Opening Of Thomas Starr King's House Of Worship, 1864
Amidst these glorious works of Thine,

The solemn minarets of the pine,
And awful Shasta's icy shrine,

Where swell Thy hymns from wave and gale,
And organ-thunders never fail,
Behind the cataract's silver veil,

Our puny walls to Thee we raise,
Our poor reed-music sounds Thy praise:
Forgive, O Lord, our childish ways!

For, kneeling on these altar-stairs,
We urge Thee not with selfish prayers,
Nor murmur at our daily cares.

Before Thee, in an evil day,
Our country's bleeding heart we lay,
And dare not ask Thy hand to stay;

But, through the war-cloud, pray to Thee
For union, but a union free,
With peace that comes of purity!

That Thou wilt bare Thy arm to, save
And, smiting through this Red Sea wave,
Make broad a pathway for the slave!

For us, confessing all our need,
We trust nor rite nor word nor deed,
Nor yet the broken staff of creed.

Assured alone that Thou art good
To each, as to the multitude,
Eternal Love and Fatherhood,

Weak, sinful, blind, to Thee we kneel,
Stretch dumbly forth our hands, and feel
Our weakness is our strong appeal.

So, by these Western gates of Even
We wait to see with Thy forgiven
The opening Golden Gate of Heaven!

Suffice it now. In time to be
Shall holier altars rise to Thee,
Thy Church our broad humanity

White flowers of love its walls shall climb,
Soft bells of peace shall ring its chime,
Its days shall all be holy time.

A sweeter song shall then be heard,

The music of the world's accord
Confessing Christ, the Inward Word!

That song shall swell from shore to shore,
One hope, one faith, one love, restore
The seamless robe that Jesus wore.

Hymn II

O Holy Father! just and true
Are all Thy works and words and ways,
And unto Thee alone are due
Thanksgiving and eternal praise!
As children of Thy gracious care,
We veil the eye, we bend the knee,
With broken words of praise and prayer,
Father and God, we come to Thee.
For Thou hast heard, O God of Right,
The sighing of the island slave;
And stretched for him the arm of might,
Not shortened that it could not save.
The laborer sits beneath his vine,
The shackled soul and hand are free;
Thanksgiving! for the work is Thine!
Praise! for the blessing is of Thee!
And oh, we feel Thy presence here,
Thy awful arm in judgment bare!
Thine eye hath seen the bondman's tear;
Thine ear hath heard the bondman's prayer.
Praise! for the pride of man is low,
The counsels of the wise are naught,
The fountains of repentance flow;
What hath our God in mercy wrought?
Speed on Thy work, Lord God of Hosts!
And when the bondman's chain is riven,
And swells from all our guilty coasts
The anthem of the free to Heaven,
Oh, not to those whom Thou hast led,
As with Thy cloud and fire before,
But. unto Thee, in fear and dread,
Be praise and glory evermore.

Lines On A Fly-Leaf

I need not ask thee, for my sake,
To read a book which well may make
Its way by native force of wit
Without my manual sign to it.
Its piquant writer needs from me
No gravely masculine guaranty,
And well might laugh her merriest laugh
At broken spears in her behalf;

Yet, spite of all the critics tell,
I frankly own I like her well.
It may be that she wields a pen
Too sharply nibbed for thin-skinned men,
That her keen arrows search and try
The armor joints of dignity,
And, though alone for error meant,
Sing through the air irreverent.
I blame her not, the young athlete
Who plants her woman's tiny feet,
And dares the chances of debate
Where bearded men might hesitate,
Who, deeply earnest, seeing well
The ludicrous and laughable,
Mingling in eloquent excess
Her anger and her tenderness,
And, chiding with a half-caress,
Strives, less for her own sex than ours,
With principalities and powers,
And points us upward to the clear
Sunned heights of her new atmosphere.

Heaven mend her faults! I will not pause
To weigh and doubt and peck at flaws,
Or waste my pity when some fool
Provokes her measureless ridicule.
Strong-minded is she? Better so
Than dulness set for sale or show,
A household folly, capped and belled
In fashion's dance of puppets held,
Or poor pretence of womanhood,
Whose formal, flavorless platitude
Is warranted from all offence
Of robust meaning's violence.
Give me the wine of thought whose head
Sparkles along the page I read,
Electric words in which I find
The tonic of the northwest wind;
The wisdom which itself allies
To sweet and pure humanities,
Where scorn of meanness, hate of wrong,
Are underlaid by love as strong;
The genial play of mirth that lights
Grave themes of thought, as when, on nights
Of summer-time, the harmless blaze
Of thunderless heat-lightning plays,
And tree and hill-top resting dim
And doubtful on the sky's vague rim,
Touched by that soft and lambent gleam,
Start sharply outlined from their dream.

Talk not to me of woman's sphere,

Nor point with Scripture texts a sneer,
Nor wrong the manliest saint of all
By doubt, if he were here, that Paul
Would own the heroines who have lent
Grace to truth's stern arbitrament,
Foregone the praise to woman sweet,
And cast their crowns at Duty's feet;
Like her, who by her strong Appeal
Made Fashion weep and Mammon feel,
Who, earliest summoned to withstand
The color-madness of the land,
Counted her life-long losses gain,
And made her own her sisters' pain;
Or her who, in her greenwood shade,
Heard the sharp call that Freedom made,
And, answering, struck from Sappho's lyre
Of love the Tyrtman carmen's fire
Or that young girl, Domremy's maid
Revived a nobler cause to aid,
Shaking from warning finger-tips
The doom of her apocalypse;
Or her, who world-wide entrance gave
To the log-cabin of the slave,
Made all his want and sorrow known,
And all earth's languages his own.

Massachusetts To Virginia

The blast from Freedom's Northern hills, upon its Southern way,
Bears greeting to Virginia from Massachusetts Bay:
No word of haughty challenging, nor battle bugle's peal,
Nor steady tread of marching files, nor clang of horsemen's steel,

No trains of deep-mouthed cannon along our highways go;
Around our silent arsenals untrodden lies the snow;
And to the land-breeze of our ports, upon their errands far,
A thousand sails of commerce swell, but none are spread for war.

We hear thy threats, Virginia! thy stormy words and high
Swell harshly on the Southern winds which melt along our sky;
Yet not one brown, hard hand foregoes its honest labor here,
No hewer of our mountain oaks suspends his axe in fear.

Wild are the waves which lash the reefs along St. George's bank;
Cold on the shores of Labrador the fog lies white and dank;
Through storm, and wave, and blinding mist, stout are the hearts which man
The fishing-smacks of Marblehead, the sea-boats of Cape Ann.

The cold north light and wintry sun glare on their icy forms,
Bent grimly o'er their straining lines or wrestling with the storms;
Free as the winds they drive before, rough as the waves they roam,
They laugh to scorn the slaver's threat against their rocky home.

What means the Old Dominion? Hath she forgot the day
When o'er her conquered valleys swept the Briton's steel array?
How, side by side with sons of hers, the Massachusetts men
Encountered Tarleton's charge of fire, and stout Cornwallis, then?

Forgets she how the Bay State, in answer to the call
Of her old House of Burgesses, spoke out from Faneuil Hall?
When, echoing back her Henry's cry, came pulsing on each breath
Of Northern winds the thrilling sounds of 'Liberty or Death!'

What asks the Old Dominion? If now her sons have proved
False to their fathers' memory, false to the faith they loved;
If she can scoff at Freedom, and its great charter spurn,
Must we of Massachusetts from truth and duty turn?

We hunt your bondmen, flying from Slavery's hateful hell;
Our voices, at your bidding, take up the bloodhound's yell;
We gather, at your summons, above our fathers' graves,
From Freedom's holy altar-horns to tear your wretched slaves!

Thank God! not yet so vilely can Massachusetts bow;
The spirit of her early time is with her even now;
Dream not because her Pilgrim blood moves slow and calm and cool,
She thus can stoop her chainless neck, a sister's slave and tool!

All that a sister State should do, all that a free State may,
Heart, hand, and purse we proffer, as in our early day;
But that one dark loathsome burden ye must stagger with alone,
And reap the bitter harvest which ye yourselves have sown!

Hold, while ye may, your struggling slaves, and burden God's free air
With woman's shriek beneath the lash, and manhood's wild despair;
Cling closer to the 'cleaving curse' that writes upon your plains
The blasting of Almighty wrath against a land of chains.

Still shame your gallant ancestry, the cavaliers of old,
By watching round the shambles where human flesh is sold;
Gloat o'er the new-born child, and count his market value, when
The maddened mother's cry of woe shall pierce the slaver's den!

Lower than plummet soundeth, sink the Virginia name;
Plant, if ye will, your fathers' graves with rankest weeds of shame;
Be, if ye will, the scandal of God's fair universe;
We wash our hands forever of your sin and shame and curse.

A voice from lips whereon the coal from Freedom's shrine hath been,
Thrilled, as but yesterday, the hearts of Berkshire's mountain men:
The echoes of that solemn voice are sadly lingering still
In all our sunny valleys, on every wind-swept hill.

And when the prowling man-thief came hunting for his prey

Beneath the very shadow of Bunker's shaft of gray,
How, through the free lips of the son, the father's warning spoke;
How, from its bonds of trade and sect, the Pilgrim city broke!

A hundred thousand right arms were lifted up on high,
A hundred thousand voices sent back their loud reply;
Through the thronged towns of Essex the startling summons rang,
And up from bench and loom and wheel her young mechanics sprang!

The voice of free, broad Middlesex, of thousands as of one,
The shaft of Bunker calling to that Lexington;
From Norfolk's ancient villages, from Plymouth's rocky bound
To where Nantucket feels the arms of ocean close to her round;

From rich and rural Worcester, where through the calm repose
Of cultured vales and fringing woods the gentle Nashua flows,
To where Wachuset's wintry blasts the mountain larches stir,
Swelled up to Heaven the thrilling cry of 'God save Latimer!'

And sandy Barnstable rose up, wet with the salt sea spray;
And Bristol sent her answering shout down Narragansett Bay!
Along the broad Connecticut old Hampden felt the thrill,
And the cheer of Hampshire's woodmen swept down from Holyoke Hill.

The voice of Massachusetts! Of her free sons and daughters,
Deep calling unto deep aloud, the sound of many waters!
Against the burden of that voice what tyrant power shall stand?
No fetters in the Bay State! No slave upon her land!

Look to it well, Virginians! In calmness we have borne,
In answer to our faith and trust, your insult and your scorn;
You've spurned our kindest counsels; you've hunted for our lives;
And shaken round our hearths and homes your manacles and gyves!

We wage no war, we lift no arm, we fling no torch within
The fire-damps of the quaking mine beneath your soil of sin;
We leave ye with your bondmen, to wrestle, while ye can,
With the strong upward tendencies and God-like soul of man!

But for us and for our children, the vow which we have given
For freedom and humanity is registered in heaven;
No slave-hunt in our borders, - no pirate on our strand!
No fetters in the Bay State, - no slave upon our land!

Mithridates At Chios
Know'st thou, O slave-cursed land!
How, when the Chian's cup of guilt
Was full to overflow, there came
God's justice in the sword of flame
That, red with slaughter to its hilt,
Blazed in the Cappadocian victor's hand?

The heavens are still and far;
But, not unheard of awful Jove,
The sighing of the island slave
Was answered, when the Ægean wave
The keels of Mithridates clove,
And the vines shrivelled in the breath of war.
'Robbers of Chios! hark,'
The victor cried, 'to Heaven's decree!
Pluck your last cluster from the vine,
Drain your last cup of Chian wine;
Slaves of your slaves, your doom shall be,
In Colchian mines by Phasis rolling dark.'
Then rose the long lament
From the hoar sea-god's dusky caves:
The priestess rent her hair and cried,
'Woe! woe! The gods are sleepless-eyed!'
And, chained and scourged, the slaves of slaves,
The lords of Chios into exile went.
'The gods at last pay well,'
So Hellas sang her taunting song,
'The fisher in his net is caught,
The Chian hath his master bought;'
And isle from isle, with laughter long,
Took up and sped the mocking parable.
Once more the slow, dumb years
Bring their avenging cycle round,
And, more than Hellas taught of old,
Our wiser lesson shall be told,
Of slaves uprising, freedom-crowned,
To break, not wield, the scourge wet with their blood and tears.

On A Prayer-Book, With its Frontispiece, Ary Scheffer's
O Ary Scheffer! when beneath thine eye,
Touched with the light that cometh from above,
Grew the sweet picture of the dear Lord's love,
No dream hadst thou that Christian hands would tear
Therefrom the token of His equal care,
And make thy symbol of His truth a lie!
The poor, dumb slave whose shackles fall away
In His compassionate gaze, grubbed smoothly out,
To mar no more the exercise devout
Of sleek oppression kneeling down to pray
Where the great oriel stains the Sabbath day!
Let whoso can before such praying-books
Kneel on his velvet cushion; I, for one,
Would sooner bow, a Parsee, to the sun,
Or tend a prayer-wheel in Thibetar brooks,
Or beat a drum on Yedo's temple-floor.
No falser idol man has bowed before,
In Indian groves or islands of the sea,
Than that which through the quaint-carved Gothic door

Looks forth, a Church without humanity!
Patron of pride, and prejudice, and wrong,
The rich man's charm and fetich of the strong,
The Eternal Fulness meted, clipped, and shorn,
The seamless robe of equal mercy torn,
The dear Christ hidden from His kindred flesh,
And, in His poor ones, crucified afresh!
Better the simple Lama scattering wide,
Where sweeps the storm Alechan's steppes along,
His paper horses for the lost to ride,
And wearying Buddha with his prayers to make
The figures living for the traveller's sake,
Than he who hopes with cheap praise to beguile
The ear of God, dishonoring man the while;
Who dreams the pearl gate's hinges, rusty grown,
Are moved by flattery's oil of tongue alone;
That in the scale Eternal Justice bears
The generous deed weighs less than selfish prayers,
And words intoned with graceful unction move
The Eternal Goodness more than lives of truth and love.
Alas, the Church! The reverend head of Jay,
Enhaloed with its saintly silvered hair,
Adorns no more the places of her prayer;
And brave young Tyng, too early called away,
Troubles the Haman of her courts no more
Like the just Hebrew at the Assyrian's door;
And her sweet ritual, beautiful but dead
As the dry husk from which the grain is shed,
And holy hymns from which the life devout
Of saints and martyrs has wellnigh gone out,
Like candles dying in exhausted air,
For Sabbath use in measured grists are ground;
And, ever while the spiritual mill goes round,
Between the upper and the nether stones,
Unseen, unheard, the wretched bondman groans,
And urges his vain plea, prayer-smothered, anthem-drowned!.
O heart of mine, keep patience!
As from the Mount of Vision, I behold,
Pure, just, and free, the Church of Christ on earth;
The martyr's dream, the golden age foretold!
And found, at last, the mystic Graal I see,
Brimmed with His blessing, pass from lip to lip
In sacred pledge of human fellowship;
And over all the songs of angels hear;
Songs of the love that casteth out all fear;
Songs of the Gospel of Humanity!
Lo! in the midst, with the same look He wore,
Healing and blessing on Genesaret's shore,
Folding together, with the all-tender might
Of His great love, the dark hands and the white,
Stands the Consoler, soothing every pain,
Making all burdens light, and breaking every chain.

Pennsylvania Hall

Not with the splendors of the days of old,
The spoil of nations, and barbaric gold;
No weapons wrested from the fields of blood,
Where dark and stern the unyielding Roman stood,
And the proud eagles of his cohorts saw
A world, war-wasted, crouching to his law;
Nor blazoned car, nor banners floating gay,
Like those which swept along the Appian Way,
When, to the welcome of imperial Rome,
The victor warrior came in triumph home,
And trumpet peal, and shoutings wild and high,
Stirred the blue quiet of the Italian sky;
But calm and grateful, prayerful and sincere,
As Christian freemen only, gathering here,
We dedicate our fair and lofty Hall,
Pillar and arch, entablature and wall,
As Virtue's shrine, as Liberty's abode,
Sacred to Freedom, and to Freedom's God!
Far statelier Halls, 'neath brighter skies than these,
Stood darkly mirrored in the Ægean seas,
Pillar and shrine, and life-like statues seen,
Graceful and pure, the marble shafts between;
Where glorious Athens from her rocky hill
Saw Art and Beauty subject to her will;
And the chaste temple, and the classic grove,
The hall of sages, and the bowers of love,
Arch, fane, and column, graced the shores, and gave
Their shadows to the blue Saronic wave;
And statelier rose, on Tiber's winding side,
The Pantheon's dome, the Coliseum's pride,
The Capitol, whose arches backward flung
The deep, clear cadence of the Roman tongue,
Whence stern decrees, like words of fate, went forth
To the awed nations of a conquered earth,
Where the proud Caesars in their glory came,
And Brutus lightened from his lips of flame!
Yet in tire porches of Athena's halls,
And in the shadow of her stately walls,
Lurked the sad bondman, and his tears of woe
Wet the cold marble with unheeded flow;
And fetters clanked beneath the silver dome
Of the proud Pantheon of imperious Rome.
Oh, not for him, the chained and stricken slave,
By Tiber's shore, or blue Ægina's wave,
In the thronged forum, or the sages' seat,
The bold lip pleaded, and the warm heart beat;
No soul of sorrow melted at his pain,
No tear of pity rusted on his chain!
But this fair Hall to Truth and Freedom given,

Pledged to the Right before all Earth and Heaven,
A free arena for the strife of mind,
To caste, or sect, or color unconfined,
Shall thrill with echoes such as ne'er of old
From Roman hall or Grecian temple rolled;
Thoughts shall find utterance such as never yet
The Propylea or the Forum met.
Beneath its roof no gladiator's strife
Shall win applauses with the waste of life;
No lordly lictor urge the barbarous game,
No wanton Lais glory in her shame.
But here the tear of sympathy shall flow,
As the ear listens to the tale of woe;
Here in stern judgment of the oppressor's wrong
Shall strong rebukings thrill on Freedom's tongue,
No partial justice hold th' unequal scale,
No pride of caste a brother's rights assail,
No tyrant's mandates echo from this wall,
Holy to Freedom and the Rights of All!
But a fair field, where mind may close with mind,
Free as the sunshine and the chainless wind;
Where the high trust is fixed on Truth alone,
And bonds and fetters from the soul are thrown;
Where wealth, and rank, and worldly pomp, and might,
Yield to the presence of the True and Right.
And fitting is it that this Hall should stand
Where Pennsylvania's Founder led his band,.
From thy blue waters, Delaware! to press
The virgin verdure of the wilderness.
Here, where all Europe with amazement saw
The soul's high freedom trammelled by no law;
Here, where the fierce and warlike forest-men
Gathered, in peace, around the home of Penn,
Awed by the weapons Love alone had given
Drawn from the holy armory of Heaven;
Where Nature's voice against the bondman's wrong
First found an earnest and indignant tongue;
Where Lay's bold message to the proud was borne;
And Keith's rebuke, and Franklin's manly scorn!
Fitting it is that here, where Freedom first
From her fair feet shook off the Old World's dust,
Spread her white pinions to our Western blast,
And her free tresses to our sunshine cast,
One Hall should rise redeemed from Slavery's ban,
One Temple sacred to the Rights of Man!
Oh! if the spirits of the parted come,
Visiting angels, to their olden home;
If the dead fathers of the land look forth
From their fair dwellings, to the things of earth,
Is it a dream, that with their eyes of love,
They gaze now on us from the bowers above?
Lay's ardent soul, and Benezet the mild,

Steadfast in faith, yet gentle as a child,
Meek-hearted Woolman, and that brother-band,
The sorrowing exiles from their 'Father land,'
Leaving their homes in Krieshiem's bowers of vine,
And the blue beauty of their glorious Rhine,
To seek amidst our solemn depths of wood
Freedom from man, and holy peace with God;
Who first of all their testimonial gave
Against the oppressor, for the outcast slave,
Is it a dream that such as these look down,
And with their blessing our rejoicings crown?
Let us rejoice, that while the pulpit's door
Is barred against the pleaders for the poor;
While the Church, wrangling upon points of faith,
Forgets her bondsmen suffering unto death;
While crafty Traffic and the lust of Gain
Unite to forge Oppression's triple chain,
One door is open, and one Temple free,
As a resting-place for hunted Liberty!
Where men may speak, unshackled and unawed,
High words of Truth, for Freedom and for God.
And when that truth its perfect work hath done,
And rich with blessings o'er our land hath gone;
When not a slave beneath his yoke shall pine,
From broad Potomac to the far Sabine:
When unto angel lips at last is given
The silver trump of Jubilee in Heaven;
And from Virginia's plains, Kentucky's shades,
And through the dim Floridian everglades,
Rises, to meet that angel-trumpet's sound,
The voice of millions from their chains unbound;
Then, though this Hall be crumbling in decay,
Its strong walls blending with the common clay,
Yet, round the ruins of its strength shall stand
The best and noblest of a ransomed land
Pilgrims, like these who throng around the shrine
Of Mecca, or of holy Palestine!
A prouder glory shall that ruin own
Than that which lingers round the Parthenon.
Here shall the child of after years be taught
The works of Freedom which his fathers wrought;
Told of the trials of the present hour,
Our weary strife with prejudice and power;
How the high errand quickened woman's soul,
And touched her lip as with a living coal;
How Freedom's martyms kept their lofty faith
True and unwavering, unto bonds and death;
The pencil's art shall sketch the ruined Hall,
The Muses' garland crown its aged wall,
And History's pen for after times record
Its consecration unto Freedom's God!

A bending staff I would not break,
A feeble faith I would not shake,
Nor even rashly pluck away
The error which some truth may stay,
Whose loss might leave the soul without
A shield against the shafts of doubt.

And yet, at times, when over all
A darker mystery seems to fall,
(May God forgive the child of dust,
Who seeks to know, where Faith should trust!)
I raise the questions, old and dark,
Of Uzdom's tempted patriarch,
And, speech-confounded, build again
The baffled tower of Shinar's plain.

I am: how little more I know!
Whence came I? Whither do I go?
A centred self, which feels and is;
A cry between the silences;
A shadow-birth of clouds at strife
With sunshine on the hills of life;
A shaft from Nature's quiver cast
Into the Future from the Past;
Between the cradle and the shroud,
A meteor's flight from cloud to cloud.

Thorough the vastness, arching all,
I see the great stars rise and fall,
The rounding seasons come and go,
The tided oceans ebb and flow;
The tokens of a central force,
Whose circles, in their widening course,
O'erlap and move the universe;
The workings of the law whence springs
The rhythmic harmony of things,
Which shapes in earth the darkling spar,
And orbs in heaven the morning star.
Of all I see, in earth and sky,
Star, flower, beast, bird, what part have I?
This conscious life, is it the same
Which thrills the universal frame,
Whereby the caverned crystal shoots,
And mounts the sap from forest roots,
Whereby the exiled wood-bird tells
When Spring makes green her native dells?
How feels the stone the pang of birth,
Which brings its sparkling prism forth?
The forest-tree the throb which gives
The life-blood to its new-born leaves?

Do bird and blossom feel, like me,
Life's many-folded mystery,
The wonder which it is to be?
Or stand I severed and distinct,
From Nature's 'chain of life' unlinked?
Allied to all, yet not the less
Prisoned in separate consciousness,
Alone o'erburdened with a sense
Of life, and cause, and consequence?

In vain to me the Sphinx propounds
The riddle of her sights and sounds;
Back still the vaulted mystery gives
The echoed question it receives.
What sings the brook? What oracle
Is in the pine-tree's organ swell?
What may the wind's low burden be?
The meaning of the moaning sea?
The hieroglyphics of the stars?
Or clouded sunset's crimson bars?
I vainly ask, for mocks my skill
The trick of Nature's cipher still.

I turn from Nature unto men,
I ask the stylus and the pen;
What sang the bards of old? What meant
The prophets of the Orient?
The rolls of buried Egypt, hid
In painted tomb and pyramid?
What mean Idumea's arrowy lines,
Or dusk Elora's monstrous signs?
How speaks the primal thought of man
From the grim carvings of Copan?

Where rests the secret? Where the keys
Of the old death-bolted mysteries?
Alas! the dead retain their trust;
Dust hath no answer from the dust.

The great enigma still unguessed,
Unanswered the eternal quest;
I gather up the scattered rays
Of wisdom in the early days,
Faint gleams and broken, like the light
Of meteors in a northern night,
Betraying to the darkling earth
The unseen sun which gave them birth;
I listen to the sibyl's chant,
The voice of priest and hierophant;
I know what Indian Kreeshna saith,
And what of life and what of death
The demon taught to Socrates;

And what, beneath his garden-trees
Slow pacing, with a dream-like tread,
The solemn-thoughted Plato said;
Nor lack I tokens, great or small,
Of God's clear light in each and all,
While holding with more dear regard
The scroll of Hebrew seer and bard,
The starry pages promise-lit
With Christ's Evangel over-writ,
Thy miracle of life and death,
O Holy One of Nazareth!

On Aztec ruins, gray and lone,
The circling serpent coils in stone,
Type of the endless and unknown;
Whereof we seek the clue to find,
With groping fingers of the blind!
Forever sought, and never found,
We trace that serpent-symbol round
Our resting-place, our starting bound
Oh, thriftlessness of dream and guess!
Oh, wisdom which is foolishness!
Why idly seek from outward things
The answer inward silence brings?
Why stretch beyond our proper sphere
And age, for that which lies so near?
Why climb the far-off hills with pain,
A nearer view of heaven to gain?
In lowliest depths of bosky dells
The hermit Contemplation dwells.
A fountain's pine-hung slope his seat,
And lotus-twined his silent feet,
Whence, piercing heaven, with screened sight,
He sees at noon the stars, whose light
Shall glorify the coining night.

Here let me pause, my quest forego;
Enough for me to feel and know
That He in whom the cause and end,
The past and future, meet and blend,
Who, girt with his Immensities,
Our vast and star-hung system sees,
Small as the clustered Pleiades,
Moves not alone the heavenly quires,
But waves the spring-time's grassy spires,
Guards not archangel feet alone,
But deigns to guide and keep my own;
Speaks not alone the words of fate
Which worlds destroy, and worlds create,
But whispers in my spirit's ear,
In tones of love, or warning fear,
A language none beside may hear.

To Him, from wanderings long and wild,
I come, an over-wearied child,
In cool and shade His peace to find,
Lice dew-fall settling on my mind.
Assured that all I know is best,
And humbly trusting for the rest,
I turn from Fancy's cloud-built scheme,
Dark creed, and mournful eastern dream
Of power, impersonal and cold,
Controlling all, itself controlled,
Maker and slave of iron laws,
Alike the subject and the cause;
From vain philosophies, that try
The sevenfold gates of mystery,
And, baffled ever, babble still,
Word-prodigal of fate and will;
From Nature, and her mockery, Art;
And book and speech of men apart,
To the still witness in my heart;
With reverence waiting to behold
His Avatar of love untold,
The Eternal Beauty new and old!

Randolph Of Roanoke

O Mother Earth! upon thy lap
Thy weary ones receiving,
And o'er them, silent as a dream,
Thy grassy mantle weaving,
Fold softly in thy long embrace
That heart so worn and broken,
And cool its pulse of fire beneath
Thy shadows old and oaken.

Shut out from him the bitter word
And serpent hiss of scorning;
Nor let the storms of yesterday
Disturb his quiet morning.
Breathe over him forgetfulness
Of all save deeds of kindness,
And, save to smiles of grateful eyes,
Press down his lids in blindness.

There, where with living ear and eye
He heard Potomac's flowing,
And, through his tall ancestral trees,
Saw autumn's sunset glowing,
He sleeps, still looking to the west,
Beneath the dark wood shadow,
As if he still would see the sun
Sink down on wave and meadow.

Bard, Sage, and Tribune! in himself
All moods of mind contrasting,
The tenderest wail of human woe,
The scorn like lightning blasting;
The pathos which from rival eyes
Unwilling tears could summon,
The stinging taunt, the fiery burst
Of hatred scarcely human!

Mirth, sparkling like a diamond shower,
From lips of life-long sadness;
Clear picturings of majestic thought
Upon a ground of madness;
And over all Romance and Song
A classic beauty throwing,
And laurelled Clio at his side
Her storied pages showing.

All parties feared him: each in turn
Beheld its schemes disjointed,
As right or left his fatal glance
And spectral finger pointed.
Sworn foe of Cant, he smote it down
With trenchant wit unsparing,
And, mocking, rent with ruthless hand
The robe Pretence was wearing.

Too honest or too proud to feign
A love he never cherished,
Beyond Virginia's border line
His patriotism perished.
While others hailed in distant skies
Our eagle's dusky pinion,
He only saw the mountain bird
Stoop o'er his Old Dominion!

Still through each change of fortune strange
Racked nerve, and brain all burning,
His loving faith in Mother-land
Knew never shade of turning;
By Britain's lakes, by Neva's tide,
Whatever sky was o'er him,
He heard her rivers' rushing sound,
Her blue peaks rose before him.

He held his slaves, yet made withal
No false and vain pretences,
Nor paid a lying priest to seek
For Scriptural defences.
His harshest words of proud rebuke,
His bitterest taunt and scorning,

Fell fire-like on the Northern brow
That bent to him in fawning.

He held his slaves; yet kept the while
His reverence for the Human;
In the dark vassals of his will
He saw but Man and Woman!
No hunter of God's outraged poor
His Roanoke valley entered;
No trader in the souls of men
Across his threshold ventured.

And when the old and wearied man
Lay down for his last sleeping,
And at his side, a slave no more,
His brother-man stood weeping,
His latest thought, his latest breath,
To Freedom's duty giving,
With failing tongue and trembling hand
The dying blest the living.

Oh, never bore his ancient State
A truer son or braver!
None trampling with a calmer scorn
On foreign hate or favor.
He knew her faults, yet never stooped
His proud and manly feeling
To poor excuses of the wrong
Or meanness of concealing.

But none beheld with clearer eye
The plague-spot o'er her spreading
None heard more sure the steps of Doom
Along her future treading.
For her as for himself he spake,
When, his gaunt frame upbracing,
He traced with dying hand 'Remorse!'
And perished in the tracing.

As from the grave where Henry sleeps,
From Vernon's weeping willow,
And from the grassy pall which hides
The Sage of Monticello,
So from the leaf-strewn burial-stone
Of Randolph's lowly dwelling,
Virginia! o'er thy land of slaves
A warning voice is swelling!

And hark! from thy deserted fields
Are sadder warnings spoken,
From quenched hearths, where thy exiled sons
Their household gods have broken.

The curse is on thee, - wolves for men,
And briers for corn-sheaves giving!
Oh, more than all thy dead renown
Were now one hero living!

Ritner

Thank God for the token! one lip is still free,
One spirit untrammelled, unbending one knee!
Like the oak of the mountain, deep-rooted and firm,
Erect, when the multitude bends to the storm;
When traitors to Freedom, and Honor, and God,
Are bowed at an Idol polluted with blood;
When the recreant North has forgotten her trust,
And the lip of her honor is low in the dust,
Thank God, that one arm from the shackle has broken!
Thank God, that one man as a freeman has spoken!
O'er thy crags, Alleghany, a blast has been blown!
Down thy tide, Susquehanna, the murmur has gone!
To the land of the South, of the charter and chain,
Of Liberty sweetened with Slavery's pain;
Where the cant of Democracy dwells on the lips
Of the forgers of fetters, and wielders of whips!
Where 'chivalric' honor means really no more
Than scourging of women, and robbing the poor!
Where the Moloch of Slavery sitteth on high,
And the words which he utters, are Worship, or die!
Right onward, oh, speed it! Wherever the blood
Of the wronged and the guiltless is crying to God;
Wherever a slave in his fetters is pining;
Wherever the lash of the driver is twining;
Wherever from kindred, torn rudely apart,
Comes the sorrowful wail of the broken of heart;
Wherever the shackles of tyranny bind,
In silence and darkness, the God-given mind;
There, God speed it onward! its truth will be felt,
The bonds shall be loosened, the iron shall melt!
And oh, will the land where the free soul of Penn
Still lingers and breathes over mountain and glen;
Will the land where a Benezet's spirit went forth
To the peeled and the meted, and outcast of Earth;
Where the words of the Charter of Liberty first
From the soul of the sage and the patriot burst;
Where first for the wronged and the weak of their kind,
The Christian and statesman their efforts combined;
Will that land of the free and the good wear a chain?
Will the call to the rescue of Freedom be vain?
No, Ritner! her 'Friends' at thy warning shall stand
Erect for the truth, like their ancestral band;
Forgetting the feuds and the strife of past time,
Counting coldness injustice, and silence a crime;
Turning back from the cavil of creeds, to unite

Once again for the poor in defence of the Right;
Breasting calmly, but firmly, the full tide of Wrong,
Overwhelmed, but not borne on its surges along;
Unappalled by the danger, the shame, and the pain,
And counting each trial for Truth as their gain!
And that bold-hearted yeomanry, honest and true,
Who, haters of fraud, give to labor its due;
Whose fathers, of old, sang in concert with thine,
On the banks of Swetara, the songs of the Rhine,
The German-born pilgrims, who first dared to brave
The scorn of the proud in the cause of the slave;
Will the sons of such men yield the lords of the South
One brow for the brand, for the padlock one mouth?
They cater to tyrants? They rivet the chain,
Which their fathers smote off, on the negro again?
No, never! one voice, like the sound in the cloud,
When the roar of the storm waxes loud and more loud,
Wherever the foot of the freeman hath pressed
From the Delaware's marge to the Lake of the West,
On the South-going breezes shall deepen and grow
Till the land it sweeps over shall tremble below!
The voice of a people, uprisen, awake,
Pennsylvania's watchword, with Freedom at stake,
Thrilling up from each valley, flung down from each height,
'Our Country and Liberty! God for the Right!'

Stanzas For The Times
Is this the land our fathers loved,
The freedom which they toiled to win?
Is this the soil whereon they moved?
Are these the graves they slumber in?
Are we the sons by whom are borne
The mantles which the dead have worn?

And shall we crouch above these graves,
With craven soul and fettered lip?
Yoke in with marked and branded slaves,
And tremble at the driver's whip?
Bend to the earth our pliant knees,
And speak but as our masters please?

Shall outraged Nature cease to feel?
Shall Mercy's tears no longer flow?
Shall ruffian threats of cord and steel,
The dungeon's gloom, the assassin's blow,
Turn back the spirit roused to save
The Truth, our Country, and the slave?

Of human skulls that shrine was made,
Round which the priests of Mexico
Before their loathsome idol prayed;

Is Freedom's altar fashioned so?
And must we yield to Freedom's God,
As offering meet, the negro's blood?

Shall tongue be mute, when deeds are wrought
Which well might shame extremest hell?
Shall freemem lock the indignant thought?
Shall Pity's bosom cease to swell?
Shall Honor bleed?- shall Truth succumb?
Shall pen, and press, and soul be dumb?

No; by each spot of haunted ground,
Where Freedom weeps her children's fall;
By Plymouth's rock, and Bunker's mound;
By Griswold's stained and shattered wall;
By Warren's ghost, by Langdon's shade;
By all the memories of our dead!

By their enlarging souls, which burst
The bands and fetters round them set;
By the free Pilgrim spirit nursed
Within our inmost bosoms, yet,
By all above, around, below,
Be ours the indignant answer,- No!

No; guided by our country's laws,
For truth, and right, and suffering man,
Be ours to strive in Freedom's cause,
As Christians may, as freemen can!
Still pouring on unwilling ears
That truth oppression only fears.

What! shall we guard our neighbor still,
While woman shrieks beneath his rod,
And while he trampels down at will
The image of a common God?
Shall watch and ward be round him set,
Of Northern nerve and bayonet?

And shall we know and share with him
The danger and the growing shame?
And see our Freedom's light grow dim,
Which should have filled the world with flame?
And, writhing, feel, where'er we turn,
A world's reproach around us burn?

Is't not enough that this is borne?
And asks our haughty neighbor more?
Must fetters which his slaves have worn
Clank round the Yankee farmer's door?
Must he be told, beside his plough,
What he must speak, and when, and how?

Must he be told his freedom stands
On Slavery's dark foundations strong;
On breaking hearts and fettered hands,
On robbery, and crime, and wrong?
That all his fathers taught is vain,-
That Freedom's emblem is the chain?

Its life, its soul, from slavery drawn!
False, foul, profane! Go, teach as well
Of holy Truth from Falsehood born!
Of Heaven refreshed by airs from Hell!
Of Virtue in the arms of Vice!
Of Demons planting Paradise!

Rail on, then, brethren of the South,
Ye shall not hear the truth the less;
No seal is on the Yankee's mouth,
No fetter on the Yankee's press!
From our Green Mountains to the sea,
One voice shall thunder, We are free!

Sumner
O Mother State! the winds of March
Blew chill o'er Auburn's Field of God,
Where, slow, beneath a leaden arch
Of sky, thy mourning children trod.

And now, with all thy woods in leaf,
Thy fields in flower, beside thy dead
Thou sittest, in thy robes of grief,
A Rachel yet uncomforted!

And once again the organ swells,
Once more the flag is half-way hung,
And yet again the mournful bells
In all thy steeple-towers are rung.

And I, obedient to thy will,
Have come a simple wreath to lay,
Superfluous, on a grave that still
Is sweet with all the flowers of May.

I take, with awe, the task assigned;
It may be that my friend might miss,
In his new sphere of heart and mind,
Some token from my band in this.

By many a tender memory moved,
Along the past my thought I send;
The record of the cause he loved

Is the best record of its friend.

No trumpet sounded in his ear,
He saw not Sinai's cloud and flame,
But never yet to Hebrew seer
A clearer voice of duty came.

God said: 'Break thou these yokes; undo
These heavy burdens. I ordain
A work to last thy whole life through,
A ministry of strife and pain.

'Forego thy dreams of lettered ease,
Put thou the scholar's promise by,
The rights of man are more than these.'
He heard, and answered: 'Here am I!'

He set his face against the blast,
His feet against the flinty shard,
Till the hard service grew, at last,
Its own exceeding great reward.

Lifted like Saul's above the crowd,
Upon his kingly forehead fell
The first sharp bolt of Slavery's cloud,
Launched at the truth he urged so well.

Ah! never yet, at rack or stake,
Was sorer loss made Freedom's gain,
Than his, who suffered for her sake
The beak-torn Titan's lingering pain!

The fixed star of his faith, through all
Loss, doubt, and peril, shone the same;
As through a night of storm, some tall,
Strong lighthouse lifts its steady flame.

Beyond the dust and smoke he saw
The sheaves of Freedom's large increase,
The holy fanes of equal law,
The New Jerusalem of peace.

The weak might fear, the worldling mock,
The faint and blind of heart regret;
All knew at last th' eternal rock
On which his forward feet were set.

The subtlest scheme of compromise
Was folly to his purpose bold;
The strongest mesh of party lies
Weak to the simplest truth he told.

One language held his heart and lip,
Straight onward to his goal he trod,
And proved the highest statesmanship
Obedience to the voice of God.

No wail was in his voice, none heard,
When treason's storm-cloud blackest grew,
The weakness of a doubtful word;
His duty, and the end, he knew.

The first to smite, the first to spare;
When once the hostile ensigns fell,
He stretched out hands of generous care
To lift the foe he fought so well.

For there was nothing base or small
Or craven in his soul's broad plan;
Forgiving all things personal,
He hated only wrong to man.

The old traditions of his State,
The memories of her great and good,
Took from his life a fresher date,
And in himself embodied stood.

How felt the greed of gold and place,
The venal crew that schemed and planned,
The fine scorn of that haughty face,
The spurning of that bribeless hand!

If than Rome's tribunes statelier
He wore his senatorial robe,
His lofty port was all for her,
The one dear spot on all the globe.

If to the master's plea he gave
The vast contempt his manhood felt,
He saw a brother in the slave,
With man as equal man he dealt.

Proud was he? If his presence kept
Its grandeur wheresoe'er he trod,
As if from Plutarch's gallery stepped
The hero and the demigod,

None failed, at least, to reach his ear,
Nor want nor woe appealed in vain;
The homesick soldier knew his cheer,
And blessed him from his ward of pain.

Safely his dearest friends may own
The slight defects he never hid,

The surface-blemish in the stone
Of the tall, stately pyramid.

Suffice it that he never brought
His conscience to the public mart;
But lived himself the truth he taught,
White-souled, clean-handed, pure of heart.

What if he felt the natural pride
Of power in noble use, too true
With thin humilities to hide
The work he did, the lore he knew?

Was he not just? Was any wronged
By that assured self-estimate?
He took but what to him belonged,
Unenvious of another's state.

Well might he heed the words he spake,
And scan with care the written page
Through which he still shall warm and wake
The hearts of men from age to age.

Ah! who shall blame him now because
He solaced thus his hours of pain!
Should not the o'erworn thresher pause,
And hold to light his golden grain?

No sense of humor dropped its oil
On the hard ways his purpose went;
Small play of fancy lightened toil;
He spake alone the thing he meant.

He loved his books, the Art that hints
A beauty veiled behind its own,
The graver's line, the pencil's tints,
The chisel's shape evoked from stone.

He cherished, void of selfish ends,
The social courtesies that bless
And sweeten life, and loved his friends
With most unworldly tenderness.

But still his tired eyes rarely learned
The glad relief by Nature brought;
Her mountain ranges never turned
His current of persistent thought.

The sea rolled chorus to his speech
Three-banked like Latium's' tall trireme,
With laboring oars; the grove and beach
Were Forum and the Academe.

The sensuous joy from all things fair
His strenuous bent of soul repressed,
And left from youth to silvered hair
Few hours for pleasure, none for rest.

For all his life was poor without,
O Nature, make the last amends
Train all thy flowers his grave about,
And make thy singing-birds his friends!

Revive again, thou summer rain,
The broken turf upon his bed
Breathe, summer wind, thy tenderest strain
Of low, sweet music overhead!

With calm and beauty symbolize
The peace which follows long annoy,
And lend our earth-bent, mourning eyes,
Some hint of his diviner joy.

For safe with right and truth he is,
As God lives he must live alway;
There is no end for souls like his,
No night for children of the day!

Nor cant nor poor solicitudes
Made weak his life's great argument;
Small leisure his for frames and moods
Who followed Duty where she went.

The broad, fair fields of God he saw
Beyond the bigot's narrow bound;
The truths he moulded into law
In Christ's beatitudes he found.

His state-craft was the Golden Rule,
His right of vote a sacred trust;
Clear, over threat and ridicule,
All heard his challenge: 'Is it just?'

And when the hour supreme had come,
Not for himself a thought he gave;
In that last pang of martyrdom,
His care was for the half-freed slave.

Not vainly dusky hands upbore,
In prayer, the passing soul to heaven
Whose mercy to His suffering poor
Was service to the Master given.

Long shall the good State's annals tell,

Her children's children long be taught,
How, praised or blamed, he guarded well
The trust he neither shunned nor sought.

If for one moment turned thy face,
O Mother, from thy son, not long
He waited calmly in his place
The sure remorse which follows wrong.

Forgiven be the State he loved
The one brief lapse, the single blot;
Forgotten be the stain removed,
Her righted record shows it not!

The lifted sword above her shield
With jealous care shall guard his fame;
The pine-tree on her ancient field
To all the winds shall speak his name.

The marble image of her son
Her loving hands shall yearly crown,
And from her pictured Pantheon
His grand, majestic face look down.

O State so passing rich before,
Who now shall doubt thy highest claim?
The world that counts thy jewels o'er
Shall longest pause at Sumner's name!

The Answer
Spare me, dread angel of reproof,
And let the sunshine weave to-day
Its gold-threads in the warp and woof
Of life so poor and gray.

Spare me awhile; the flesh is weak.
These lingering feet, that fain would stray
Among the flowers, shall some day seek
The strait and narrow way.

Take off thy ever-watchful eye,
The awe of thy rebuking frown;
The dullest slave at times must sigh
To fling his burdens down;

To drop his galley's straining oar,
And press, in summer warmth and calm,
The lap of some enchanted shore
Of blossom and of balm.

Grudge not my life its hour of bloom,

My heart its taste of long desire;
This day be mine: be those to come
As duty shall require.

The deep voice answered to my own,
Smiting my selfish prayers away;
'To-morrow is with God alone,
And man hath but to-day.

'Say not, thy fond, vain heart within,
The Father's arm shall still be wide,
When from these pleasant ways of sin
Thou turn'st at eventide.

''Cast thyself down,' the tempter saith,
'And angels shall thy feet upbear.'
He bids thee make a lie of faith,
And blasphemy of prayer.

'Though God be good and free be heaven,
No force divine can love compel;
And, though the song of sins forgiven
May sound through lowest hell,

'The sweet persuasion of His voice
Respects thy sanctity of will.
He giveth day: thou hast thy choice
To walk in darkness still;

'As one who, turning from the light,
Watches his own gray shadow fall,
Doubting, upon his path of night,
If there be day at all!

'No word of doom may shut thee out,
No wind of wrath may downward whirl,
No swords of fire keep watch about
The open gates of pearl;

'A tenderer light than moon or sun,
Than song of earth a sweeter hymn,
May shine and sound forever on,
And thou be deaf and dim.

'Forever round the Mercy-seat
The guiding lights of Love shall burn;
But what if, habit-bound, thy feet
Shall lack the will to turn?

'What if thine eye refuse to see,
Thine ear of Heaven's free welcome fail,
And thou a willing captive be,

Thyself thy own dark jail?

'Oh, doom beyond the saddest guess,
As the long years of God unroll,
To make thy dreary selfishness
The prison of a soul!

'To doubt the love that fain would break
The fetters from thy self-bound limb;
And dream that God can thee forsake
As thou forsakest Him!'

The Bartholdi Statue

The land, that, from the rule of kings,
In freeing us, itself made free,
Our Old World Sister, to us brings
Her sculptured Dream of Liberty,

Unlike the shapes on Egypt's sands
Uplifted by the toil-worn,
On Freedom's soil with freemen's hands
We rear the symbol free hands gave.

O France, the beautiful! to thee
Once more a debt of love we owe
In peace beneath thy Colors Three,
We hail a later Rochambeau!

Rise, stately Symbol! holding forth
Thy light and hope to all who sit
In chains and darkness! Belt the earth
With watch-fires from thy torch uplit!

Reveal the primal mandate still
Which Chaos heard and ceased to be,
Trace on mid-air th' Eternal Will
In signs of fire: 'Let man be free!'

Shine far, shine free, a guiding light
To Reason's ways and Virtue's aim,
A lightning-flash the wretch to smite
Who shields his license with thy name!

The Branded Hand

Welcome home again, brave seaman! with thy thoughtful brow and gray,
And the old heroic spirit of our earlier, better day;
With that front of calm endurance, on whose steady nerve in vain
Pressed the iron of the prison, smote the fiery shafts of pain!
Is the tyrant's brand upon thee? Did the brutal cravens aim
To make God's truth thy falsehood, His holiest work thy shame?

When, all blood-quenched, from the torture the iron was withdrawn,
How laughed their evil angel the baffled fools to scorn!
They change to wrong the duty which God hath written out
On the great heart of humanity, too legible for doubt!
They, the loathsome moral lepers, blotched from footsole up to crown,
Give to shame what God hath given unto honor and renown!
Why, that brand is highest honor! than its traces never yet
Upon old armorial hatchments was a prouder blazon set;
And thy unborn generations, as they tread our rocky strand,
Shall tell with pride the story of their father's branded hand!
As the Templar home was welcome, bearing back from Syrian wars
The scars of Arab lances and of Paynim scimitars,
The pallor of the prison, and the shackle's crimson span,
So we meet thee, so we greet thee, truest friend of God and man.
He suffered for the ransom of the dear Redeemer's grave,
Thou for His living presence in the bound and bleeding slave;
He for a soil no longer by the feet of angels trod,
Thou for the true Shechinah, the present home of God!
For, while the jurist, sitting with the slave-whip o'er him swung,
From the tortured truths of freedom the lie of slavery wrung,
And the solemn priest to Moloch, on each God-deserted shrine,
Broke the bondman's heart for bread, poured the bondman's blood for wine;
While the multitude in blindness to a far-off Saviour knelt
And spurned, the while, the temple where a present Saviour dwelt;
Thou beheld'st Him in the task-field, in the prison shadows dim,
And thy mercy to the bondman, it was mercy unto Him!
In thy lone and long night-watches, sky above and wave below,
Thou didst learn a higher wisdom than the babbling schoolmen know;
God's stars and silence taught thee, as His angels only can,
That the one sole sacred thing beneath the cope of heaven is Man!
That he who treads profanely on the scrolls of law and creed,
In the depth of God's great goodness may find mercy in his need;
But woe to him who crushes the soul with chain and rod,
And herds with lower natures the awful form of God!.
Then lift that manly right-hand, bold ploughman of the wave!
Its branded palm shall prophesy, 'Salvation to the Slave!'
Hold up its fire-wrought language, that whoso reads may feel
His heart swell strong within him, his sinews change to steel.
Hold it up before our sunshine, up against our Northern air;
Ho! men of Massachusetts, for the love of God, look there!
Take it henceforth for your standard, like the Bruce's heart of yore,
In the dark strife closing round ye, let that hand be seen before!
And the masters of the slave-land shall tremble at that sign,
When it points its finger Southward along the Puritan line
Can the craft of State avail them? Can a Christless church withstand,
In the van of Freedom's onset, the coming of that hand?

The Bridal Of Pennacook
We had been wandering for many days
Through the rough northern country. We had seen
The sunset, with its bars of purple cloud,

Like a new heaven, shine upward from the lake
Of Winnepiseogee; and had felt
The sunrise breezes, midst the leafy isles
Which stoop their summer beauty to the lips
Of the bright waters. We had checked our steeds,
Silent with wonder, where the mountain wall
Is piled to heaven; and, through the narrow rift
Of the vast rocks, against whose rugged feet
Beats the mad torrent with perpetual roar,
Where noonday is as twilight, and the wind
Comes burdened with the everlasting moan
Of forests and of far-off waterfalls,
We had looked upward where the summer sky,
Tasselled with clouds light-woven by the sun,
Sprung its blue arch above the abutting crags
O'er-roofing the vast portal of the land
Beyond the wall of mountains. We had passed
The high source of the Saco; and bewildered
In the dwarf spruce-belts of the Crystal Hills,
Had heard above us, like a voice in the cloud,
The horn of Fabyan sounding; and atop
Of old Agioochook had seen the mountains'
Piled to the northward, shagged with wood, and thick
As meadow mole-hills, the far sea of Casco,
A white gleam on the horizon of the east;
Fair lakes, embosomed in the woods and hills;
Moosehillock's mountain range, and Kearsarge
Lifting his granite forehead to the sun!

And we had rested underneath the oaks
Shadowing the bank, whose grassy spires are shaken
By the perpetual beating of the falls
Of the wild Ammonoosuc. We had tracked
The winding Pemigewasset, overhung
By beechen shadows, whitening down its rocks,
Or lazily gliding through its intervals,
From waving rye-fields sending up the gleam
Of sunlit waters. We had seen the moon
Rising behind Umbagog's eastern pines,
Like a great Indian camp-fire; and its beams
At midnight spanning with a bridge of silver
The Merrimac by Uncanoonuc's falls.

There were five souls of us whom travel's chance
Had thrown together in these wild north hills
A city lawyer, for a month escaping
From his dull office, where the weary eye
Saw only hot brick walls and close thronged streets;
Briefless as yet, but with an eye to see
Life's sunniest side, and with a heart to take
Its chances all as godsends; and his brother,
Pale from long pulpit studies, yet retaining

The warmth and freshness of a genial heart,
Whose mirror of the beautiful and true,
In Man and Nature, was as yet undimmed
By dust of theologic strife, or breath
Of sect, or cobwebs of scholastic lore;
Like a clear crystal calm of water, taking
The hue and image of o'erleaning flowers,
Sweet human faces, white clouds of the noon,
Slant starlight glimpses through the dewy leaves,
And tenderest moonrise. 'Twas, in truth, a study,
To mark his spirit, alternating between
A decent and professional gravity
And an irreverent mirthfulness, which often
Laughed in the face of his divinity,
Plucked off the sacred ephod, quite unshrined
The oracle, and for the pattern priest
Left us the man. A shrewd, sagacious merchant,
To whom the soiled sheet found in Crawford's inn,
Giving the latest news of city stocks
And sales of cotton, had a deeper meaning
Than the great presence of the awful mountains
Glorified by the sunset; and his daughter,
A delicate flower on whom had blown too long
Those evil winds, which, sweeping from the ice
And winnowing the fogs of Labrador,
Shed their cold blight round Massachusetts Bay,
With the same breath which stirs Spring's opening leaves
And lifts her half-formed flower-bell on its stem,
Poisoning our seaside atmosphere.

It chanced that as we turned upon our homeward way,
A drear northeastern storm came howling up
The valley of the Saco; and that girl
Who had stood with us upon Mount Washington,
Her brown locks ruffled by the wind which whirled
In gusts around its sharp, cold pinnacle,
Who had joined our gay trout-fishing in the streams
Which lave that giant's feet; whose laugh was heard
Like a bird's carol on the sunrise breeze
Which swelled our sail amidst the lake's green islands,
Shrank from its harsh, chill breath, and visibly drooped
Like a flower in the frost. So, in that quiet inn
Which looks from Conway on the mountains piled
Heavily against the horizon of the north,
Like summer thunder-clouds, we made our home
And while the mist hung over dripping hills,
And the cold wind-driven rain-drops all day long
Beat their sad music upon roof and pane,
We strove to cheer our gentle invalid.

The lawyer in the pauses of the storm
Went angling down the Saco, and, returning,

Recounted his adventures and mishaps;
Gave us the history of his scaly clients,
Mingling with ludicrous yet apt citations
Of barbarous law Latin, passages
From Izaak Walton's Angler, sweet and fresh
As the flower-skirted streams of Staffordshire,
Where, under aged trees, the southwest wind
Of soft June mornings fanned the thin, white hair
Of the sage fisher. And, if truth be told,
Our youthful candidate forsook his sermons,
His commentaries, articles and creeds,
For the fair page of human loveliness,
The missal of young hearts, whose sacred text
Is music, its illumining, sweet smiles.
He sang the songs she loved; and in his low,
Deep, earnest voice, recited many a page
Of poetry, the holiest, tenderest lines
Of the sad bard of Olney, the sweet songs,
Simple and beautiful as Truth and Nature,
Of him whose whitened locks on Rydal Mount
Are lifted yet by morning breezes blowing
From the green hills, immortal in his lays.
And for myself, obedient to her wish,
I searched our landlord's proffered library,
A well-thumbed Bunyan, with its nice wood pictures
Of scaly fiends and angels not unlike them;
Watts' unmelodious psalms; Astrology's
Last home, a musty pile of almanacs,
And an old chronicle of border wars
And Indian history. And, as I read
A story of the marriage of the Chief
Of Saugus to the dusky Weetamoo,
Daughter of Passaconaway, who dwelt
In the old time upon the Merrimac,
Our fair one, in the playful exercise
Of her prerogative, the right divine
Of youth and beauty, bade us versify
The legend, and with ready pencil sketched
Its plan and outlines, laughingly assigning
To each his part, and barring our excuses
With absolute will. So, like the cavaliers
Whose voices still are heard in the Romance
Of silver-tongued Boccaccio, on the banks
Of Arno, with soft tales of love beguiling
The ear of languid beauty, plague-exiled
From stately Florence, we rehearsed our rhymes
To their fair auditor, and shared by turns
Her kind approval and her playful censure.

It may be that these fragments owe alone
To the fair setting of their circumstances,
The associations of time, scene, and audience,

Their place amid the pictures which fill up
The chambers of my memory. Yet I trust
That some, who sigh, while wandering in thought,
Pilgrims of Romance o'er the olden world,
That our broad land, our sea-like lakes and mountains
Piled to the clouds, our rivers overhung
By forests which have known no other change
For ages than the budding and the fall
Of leaves, our valleys lovelier than those
Which the old poets sang of, should but figure
On the apocryphal chart of speculation
As pastures, wood-lots, mill-sites, with the privileges,
Rights, and appurtenances, which make up
A Yankee Paradise, unsung, unknown,
To beautiful tradition; even their names,
Whose melody yet lingers like the last
Vibration of the red man's requiem,
Exchanged for syllables significant,
Of cotton-mill and rail-car, will look kindly
Upon this effort to call up the ghost
Of our dim Past, and listen with pleased ear
To the responses of the questioned Shade.

I. THE MERRIMAC

O child of that white-crested mountain whose springs
Gush forth in the shade of the cliff-eagle's wings,
Down whose slopes to the lowlands thy wild waters shine,
Leaping gray walls of rock, flashing through the dwarf pine;
From that cloud-curtained cradle so cold and so lone,
From the arms of that wintry-locked mother of stone,
By hills hung with forests, through vales wide and free,
Thy mountain-born brightness glanced down to the sea.

No bridge arched thy waters save that where the trees
Stretched their long arms above thee and kissed in the breeze:
No sound save the lapse of the waves on thy shores,
The plunging of otters, the light dip of oars.

Green-tufted, oak-shaded, by Amoskeag's fall
Thy twin Uncanoonucs rose stately and tall,
Thy Nashua meadows lay green and unshorn,
And the hills of Pentucket were tasselled with corn.
But thy Pennacook valley was fairer than these,
And greener its grasses and taller its trees,
Ere the sound of an axe in the forest had rung,
Or the mower his scythe in the meadows had swung.

In their sheltered repose looking out from the wood
The bark-builded wigwams of Pennacook stood;
There glided the corn-dance, the council-fire shone,
And against the red war-post the hatchet was thrown.

There the old smoked in silence their pipes, and the young
To the pike and the white-perch their baited lines flung;
There the boy shaped his arrows, and there the shy maid
Wove her many-hued baskets and bright wampum braid.

O Stream of the Mountains! if answer of thine
Could rise from thy waters to question of mine,
Methinks through the din of thy thronged banks a moan
Of sorrow would swell for the days which have gone.

Not for thee the dull jar of the loom and the wheel,
The gliding of shuttles, the ringing of steel;
But that old voice of waters, of bird and of breeze,
The dip of the wild-fowl, the rustling of trees.

II. THE BASHABA

Lift we the twilight curtains of the Past,
And, turning from familiar sight and sound,
Sadly and full of reverence let us cast
A glance upon Tradition's shadowy ground,
Led by the few pale lights which, glimmering round
That dim, strange land of Eld, seem dying fast;
And that which history gives not to the eye,
The faded coloring of Time's tapestry,
Let Fancy, with her dream-dipped brush, supply.

Roof of bark and walls of pine,
Through whose chinks the sunbeams shine,
Tracing many a golden line
On the ample floor within;
Where, upon that earth-floor stark,
Lay the gaudy mats of bark,
With the bear's hide, rough and dark,
And the red-deer's skin.

Window-tracery, small and slight,
Woven of the willow white,
Lent a dimly checkered light;
And the night-stars glimmered down,
Where the lodge-fire's heavy smoke,
Slowly through an opening broke,
In the low roof, ribbed with oak,
Sheathed with hemlock brown.

Gloomed behind the changeless shade
By the solemn pine-wood made;
Through the rugged palisade,
In the open foreground planted,
Glimpses came of rowers rowing,
Stir of leaves and wild-flowers blowing,
Steel-like gleams of water flowing,
In the sunlight slanted.

Here the mighty Bashaba
Held his long-unquestioned sway,
From the White Hills, far away,
To the great sea's sounding shore;
Chief of chiefs, his regal word
All the river Sachems heard,
At his call the war-dance stirred,
Or was still once more.

There his spoils of chase and war,
Jaw of wolf and black bear's paw,
Panther's skin and eagle's claw,
Lay beside his axe and bow;
And, adown the roof-pole hung,
Loosely on a snake-skin strung,
In the smoke his scalp-locks swung
Grimly to and fro.

Nightly down the river going,
Swifter was the hunter's rowing,
When he saw that lodge-fire, glowing
O'er the waters still and red;
And the squaw's dark eye burned brighter,
And she drew her blanket tighter,
As, with quicker step and lighter,
From that door she fled.

For that chief had magic skill,
And a Panisee's dark will,
Over powers of good and ill,
Powers which bless and powers which ban;
Wizard lord of Pennacook,
Chiefs upon their war-path shook,
When they met the steady look
Of that wise dark man.

Tales of him the gray squaw told,
When the winter night-wind cold
Pierced her blanket's thickest fold,
And her fire burned low and small,
Till the very child abed,
Drew its bear-skin over bead,
Shrinking from the pale lights shed
On the trembling wall.

All the subtle spirits hiding
Under earth or wave, abiding
In the caverned rock, or riding
Misty clouds or morning breeze;
Every dark intelligence,
Secret soul, and influence

Of all things which outward sense
Feels, or bears, or sees,

These the wizard's skill confessed,
At his bidding banned or blessed,
Stormful woke or lulled to rest
Wind and cloud, and fire and flood;
Burned for him the drifted snow,
Bade through ice fresh lilies blow,
And the leaves of summer grow
Over winter's wood!

Not untrue that tale of old!
Now, as then, the wise and bold
All the powers of Nature hold
Subject to their kingly will;
From the wondering crowds ashore,
Treading life's wild waters o'er,
As upon a marble floor,
Moves the strong man still.

Still, to such, life's elements
With their sterner laws dispense,
And the chain of consequence
Broken in their pathway lies;
Time and change their vassals making,
Flowers from icy pillows waking,
Tresses of the sunrise shaking
Over midnight skies.
Still, to th' earnest soul, the sun
Rests on towered Gibeon,
And the moon of Ajalon
Lights the battle-grounds of life;
To his aid the strong reverses
Hidden powers and giant forces,
And the high stars, in their courses,
Mingle in his strife!

III. THE DAUGHTER
The soot-black brows of men, the yell
Of women thronging round the bed,
The tinkling charm of ring and shell,
The Powah whispering o'er the dead!

All these the Sachem's home had known,
When, on her journey long and wild
To the dim World of Souls, alone,
In her young beauty passed the mother of his child.

Three bow-shots from the Sachem's dwelling
They laid her in the walnut shade,
Where a green hillock gently swelling

Her fitting mound of burial made.
There trailed the vine in summer hours,
The tree-perched squirrel dropped his shell,
On velvet moss and pale-hued flowers,
Woven with leaf and spray, the softened sunshine fell!

The Indian's heart is hard and cold,
It closes darkly o'er its care,
And formed in Nature's sternest mould,
Is slow to feel, and strong to bear.
The war-paint on the Sachem's face,
Unwet with tears, shone fierce and red,
And still, in battle or in chase,
Dry leaf and snow-rime crisped beneath his foremost tread.

Yet when her name was heard no more,
And when the robe her mother gave,
And small, light moccasin she wore,
Had slowly wasted on her grave,
Unmarked of him the dark maids sped
Their sunset dance and moonlit play;
No other shared his lonely bed,
No other fair young head upon his bosom lay.

A lone, stern man. Yet, as sometimes
The tempest-smitten tree receives
From one small root the sap which climbs
Its topmost spray and crowning leaves,
So from his child the Sachem drew
A life of Love and Hope, and felt
His cold and rugged nature through
The softness and the warmth of her young being melt.

A laugh which in the woodland rang
Bemocking April's gladdest bird,—
A light and graceful form which sprang
To meet him when his step was heard,
Eyes by his lodge-fire flashing dark,
Small fingers stringing bead and shell
Or weaving mats of bright-hued bark,
With these the household-god had graced his wigwam well.

Child of the forest! strong and free,
Slight-robed, with loosely flowing hair,
She swam the lake or climbed the tree,
Or struck the flying bird in air.
O'er the heaped drifts of winter's moon
Her snow-shoes tracked the hunter's way;
And dazzling in the summer noon
The blade of her light oar threw off its shower of spray!

Unknown to her the rigid rule,

The dull restraint, the chiding frown,
The weary torture of the school,
The taming of wild nature down.
Her only lore, the legends told
Around the hunter's fire at night;
Stars rose and set, and seasons rolled,
Flowers bloomed and snow-flakes fell, unquestioned in her sight.

Unknown to her the subtle skill
With which the artist-eye can trace
In rock and tree and lake and hill
The outlines of divinest grace;
Unknown the fine soul's keen unrest,
Which sees, admires, yet yearns alway;
Too closely on her mother's breast
To note her smiles of love the child of Nature lay!

It is enough for such to be
Of common, natural things a part,
To feel, with bird and stream and tree,
The pulses of the same great heart;
But we, from Nature long exiled,
In our cold homes of Art and Thought
Grieve like the stranger-tended child,
Which seeks its mother's arms, and sees but feels them not.

The garden rose may richly bloom
In cultured soil and genial air,
To cloud the light of Fashion's room
Or droop in Beauty's midnight hair;
In lonelier grace, to sun and dew
The sweetbrier on the hillside shows
Its single leaf and fainter hue,
Untrained and wildly free, yet still a sister rose!

Thus o'er the heart of Weetamoo
Their mingling shades of joy and ill
The instincts of her nature threw;
The savage was a woman still.
Midst outlines dim of maiden schemes,
Heart-colored prophecies of life,
Rose on the ground of her young dreams
The light of a new home, the lover and the wife.

IV. THE WEDDING

Cool and dark fell the autumn night,
But the Bashaba's wigwam glowed with light,
For down from its roof, by green withes hung,
Flaring and smoking the pine-knots swung.

And along the river great wood-fires
Shot into the night their long, red spires,

Showing behind the tall, dark wood,
Flashing before on the sweeping flood.

In the changeful wind, with shimmer and shade,
Now high, now low, that firelight played,
On tree-leaves wet with evening dews,
On gliding water and still canoes.

The trapper that night on Turee's brook,
And the weary fisher on Contoocook,
Saw over the marshes, and through the pine,
And down on the river, the dance-lights shine.
For the Saugus Sachem had come to woo
The Bashaba's daughter Weetamoo,
And laid at her father's feet that night
His softest furs and wampum white.

From the Crystal Hills to the far southeast
The river Sagamores came to the feast;
And chiefs whose homes the sea-winds shook
Sat down on the mats of Pennacook.

They came from Sunapee's shore of rock,
From the snowy sources of Snooganock,
And from rough Coos whose thick woods shake
Their pine-cones in Umbagog Lake.

From Ammonoosuc's mountain pass,
Wild as his home, came Chepewass;
And the Keenomps of the bills which throw
Their shade on the Smile of Manito.

With pipes of peace and bows unstrung,
Glowing with paint came old and young,
In wampum and furs and feathers arrayed,
To the dance and feast the Bashaba made.

Bird of the air and beast of the field,
All which the woods and the waters yield,
On dishes of birch and hemlock piled,
Garnished and graced that banquet wild.

Steaks of the brown bear fat and large
From the rocky slopes of the Kearsarge;
Delicate trout from Babboosuck brook,
And salmon speared in the Contoocook;

Squirrels which fed where nuts fell thick
in the gravelly bed of the Otternic;
And small wild-hens in reed-snares caught
from the banks of Sondagardee brought;

Pike and perch from the Suncook taken,
Nuts from the trees of the Black Hills shaken,
Cranberries picked in the Squamscot bog,
And grapes from the vines of Piscataquog:

And, drawn from that great stone vase which stands
In the river scooped by a spirit's hands,
Garnished with spoons of shell and horn,
Stood the birchen dishes of smoking corn.

Thus bird of the air and beast of the field,
All which the woods and the waters yield,
Furnished in that olden day
The bridal feast of the Bashaba.

And merrily when that feast was done
On the fire-lit green the dance begun,
With squaws' shrill stave, and deeper hum
Of old men beating the Indian drum.

Painted and plumed, with scalp-locks flowing,
And red arms tossing and black eyes glowing,
Now in the light and now in the shade
Around the fires the dancers played.

The step was quicker, the song more shrill,
And the beat of the small drums louder still
Whenever within the circle drew
The Saugus Sachem and Weetamoo.

The moons of forty winters had shed
Their snow upon that chieftain's head,
And toil and care and battle's chance
Had seamed his hard, dark countenance.

A fawn beside the bison grim,
Why turns the bride's fond eye on him,
In whose cold look is naught beside
The triumph of a sullen pride?

Ask why the graceful grape entwines
The rough oak with her arm of vines;
And why the gray rock's rugged cheek
The soft lips of the mosses seek.

Why, with wise instinct, Nature seems
To harmonize her wide extremes,
Linking the stronger with the weak,
The haughty with the soft and meek!

V. THE NEW HOME
A wild and broken landscape, spiked with firs,

Roughening the bleak horizon's northern edge;
Steep, cavernous hillsides, where black hemlock spurs
And sharp, gray splinters of the wind-swept ledge
Pierced the thin-glazed ice, or bristling rose,
Where the cold rim of the sky sunk down upon the snows.

And eastward cold, wide marshes stretched away,
Dull, dreary flats without a bush or tree,
O'er-crossed by icy creeks, where twice a day
Gurgled the waters of the moon-struck sea;
And faint with distance came the stifled roar,
The melancholy lapse of waves on that low shore.

No cheerful village with its mingling smokes,
No laugh of children wrestling in the snow,
No camp-fire blazing through the hillside oaks,
No fishers kneeling on the ice below;
Yet midst all desolate things of sound and view,
Through the long winter moons smiled dark-eyed Weetamoo.

Her heart had found a home; and freshly all
Its beautiful affections overgrew
Their rugged prop. As o'er some granite wall
Soft vine-leaves open to the moistening dew
And warm bright sun, the love of that young wife
Found on a hard cold breast the dew and warmth of life.

The steep, bleak hills, the melancholy shore,
The long, dead level of the marsh between,
A coloring of unreal beauty wore
Through the soft golden mist of young love seen.
For o'er those hills and from that dreary plain,
Nightly she welcomed home her hunter chief again.

No warmth of heart, no passionate burst of feeling,
Repaid her welcoming smile and parting kiss,
No fond and playful dalliance half concealing,
Under the guise of mirth, its tenderness;

But, in their stead, the warrior's settled pride,
And vanity's pleased smile with homage satisfied.

Enough for Weetamoo, that she alone
Sat on his mat and slumbered at his side;
That he whose fame to her young ear had flown
Now looked upon her proudly as his bride;
That he whose name the Mohawk trembling heard
Vouchsafed to her at times a kindly look or word.

For she had learned the maxims of her race,
Which teach the woman to become a slave,
And feel herself the pardonless disgrace

Of love's fond weakness in the wise and brave,
The scandal and the shame which they incur,
Who give to woman all which man requires of her.

So passed the winter moons. The sun at last
Broke link by link the frost chain of the rills,
And the warm breathings of the southwest passed
Over the hoar rime of the Saugus hills;
The gray and desolate marsh grew green once more,
And the birch-tree's tremulous shade fell round the Sachem's door.

Then from far Pennacook swift runners came,
With gift and greeting for the Saugus chief;
Beseeching him in the great Sachem's name,
That, with the coming of the flower and leaf,
The song of birds, the warm breeze and the rain,
Young Weetamoo might greet her lonely sire again.

And Winnepurkit called his chiefs together,
And a grave council in his wigwam met,
Solemn and brief in words, considering whether
The rigid rules of forest etiquette
Permitted Weetamoo once more to look
Upon her father's face and green-banked Pennacook.

With interludes of pipe-smoke and strong water,
The forest sages pondered, and at length,
Concluded in a body to escort her
Up to her father's home of pride and strength,
Impressing thus on Pennacook a sense
Of Winnepurkit's power and regal consequence.

So through old woods which Aukeetamit's hand,
A soft and many-shaded greenness lent,
Over high breezy hills, and meadow land
Yellow with flowers, the wild procession went,
Till, rolling down its wooded banks between,
A broad, clear, mountain stream, the Merrimac was seen.

The hunter leaning on his bow undrawn,
The fisher lounging on the pebbled shores,
Squaws in the clearing dropping the seed-corn,
Young children peering through the wigwam doors,
Saw with delight, surrounded by her train
Of painted Saugus braves, their Weetamoo again.

VI. AT PENNACOOK
The hills are dearest which our childish feet
Have climbed the earliest; and the streams most sweet
Are ever those at which our young lips drank,
Stooped to their waters o'er the grassy bank.

Midst the cold dreary sea-watch, Home's hearth-light
Shines round the helmsman plunging through the night;
And still, with inward eye, the traveller sees
In close, dark, stranger streets his native trees.

The home-sick dreamer's brow is nightly fanned
By breezes whispering of his native land,
And on the stranger's dim and dying eye
The soft, sweet pictures of his childhood lie.

Joy then for Weetamoo, to sit once more
A child upon her father's wigwam floor!
Once more with her old fondness to beguile
From his cold eye the strange light of a smile.

The long, bright days of summer swiftly passed,
The dry leaves whirled in autumn's rising blast,
And evening cloud and whitening sunrise rime
Told of the coming of the winter-time.

But vainly looked, the while, young Weetamoo,
Down the dark river for her chief's canoe;
No dusky messenger from Saugus brought
The grateful tidings which the young wife sought.

At length a runner from her father sent,
To Winnepurkit's sea-cooled wigwam went
'Eagle of Saugus, in the woods the dove
Mourns for the shelter of thy wings of love.'

But the dark chief of Saugus turned aside
In the grim anger of hard-hearted pride;
I bore her as became a chieftain's daughter,
Up to her home beside the gliding water.

If now no more a mat for her is found
Of all which line her father's wigwam round,
Let Pennacook call out his warrior train,
And send her back with wampum gifts again.'

The baffled runner turned upon his track,
Bearing the words of Winnepurkit back.
'Dog of the Marsh,' cried Pennacook, 'no more
Shall child of mine sit on his wigwam floor.

'Go, let him seek some meaner squaw to spread
The stolen bear-skin of his beggar's bed;
Son of a fish-hawk! let him dig his clams
For some vile daughter of the Agawams,

'Or coward Nipmucks! may his scalp dry black
In Mohawk smoke, before I send her back.'

He shook his clenched hand towards the ocean wave,
While hoarse assent his listening council gave.

Alas poor bride! can thy grim sire impart
His iron hardness to thy woman's heart?
Or cold self-torturing pride like his atone
For love denied and life's warm beauty flown?

On Autumn's gray and mournful grave the snow
Hung its white wreaths; with stifled voice and low
The river crept, by one vast bridge o'er-crossed,
Built by the boar-locked artisan of Frost.

And many a moon in beauty newly born
Pierced the red sunset with her silver horn,
Or, from the east, across her azure field
Rolled the wide brightness of her full-orbed shield.

Yet Winnepurkit came not,—on the mat
Of the scorned wife her dusky rival sat;
And he, the while, in Western woods afar,
Urged the long chase, or trod the path of war.

Dry up thy tears, young daughter of a chief!
Waste not on him the sacredness of grief;
Be the fierce spirit of thy sire thine own,
His lips of scorning, and his heart of stone.

What heeds the warrior of a hundred fights,
The storm-worn watcher through long hunting nights,
Cold, crafty, proud of woman's weak distress,
Her home-bound grief and pining loneliness?

VII. THE DEPARTURE

The wild March rains had fallen fast and long
The snowy mountains of the North among,
Making each vale a watercourse, each hill
Bright with the cascade of some new-made rill.

Gnawed by the sunbeams, softened by the rain,
Heaved underneath by the swollen current's strain,
The ice-bridge yielded, and the Merrimac
Bore the huge ruin crashing down its track.

On that strong turbid water, a small boat
Guided by one weak hand was seen to float;
Evil the fate which loosed it from the shore,
Too early voyager with too frail an oar!

Down the vexed centre of that rushing tide,
The thick huge ice-blocks threatening either side,
The foam-white rocks of Amoskeag in view,

With arrowy swiftness sped that light canoe.

The trapper, moistening his moose's meat
On the wet bank by Uncanoonuc's feet,
Saw the swift boat flash down the troubled stream;
Slept he, or waked he? was it truth or dream?

The straining eye bent fearfully before,
The small hand clenching on the useless oar,
The bead-wrought blanket trailing o'er the water
He knew them all—woe for the Sachem's daughter!

Sick and aweary of her lonely life,
Heedless of peril, the still faithful wife
Had left her mother's grave, her father's door,
To seek the wigwam of her chief once more.

Down the white rapids like a sear leaf whirled,
On the sharp rocks and piled-up ices hurled,
Empty and broken, circled the canoe
In the vexed pool below—but where was Weetamoo.

VIII. SONG OF INDIAN WOMEN
The Dark eye has left us,
The Spring-bird has flown;
On the pathway of spirits
She wanders alone.
The song of the wood-dove has died on our shore
Mat wonck kunna-monee! We hear it no more!

O dark water Spirit
We cast on thy wave
These furs which may never
Hang over her grave;
Bear down to the lost one the robes that she wore
Mat wonck kunna-monee! We see her no more!

Of the strange land she walks in
No Powah has told:
It may burn with the sunshine,
Or freeze with the cold.
Let us give to our lost one the robes that she wore:
Mat wonck kunna-monee! We see her no more!

The path she is treading
Shall soon be our own;
Each gliding in shadow
Unseen and alone!
In vain shall we call on the souls gone before:
Mat wonck kunna-monee! They hear us no more!

O mighty Sowanna!

Thy gateways unfold,
From thy wigwam of sunset
Lift curtains of gold!

Take home the poor Spirit whose journey is o'er
Mat wonck kunna-monee! We see her no more!

So sang the Children of the Leaves beside
The broad, dark river's coldly flowing tide;
Now low, now harsh, with sob-like pause and swell,
On the high wind their voices rose and fell.
Nature's wild music, sounds of wind-swept trees,
The scream of birds, the wailing of the breeze,
The roar of waters, steady, deep, and strong,
Mingled and murmured in that farewell song.

The Christian Slave

A christian! going, gone!
Who bids for God's own image? for his grace,
Which that poor victim of the market-place
Hath in her suffering won?
My God! can such things be?
Hast Thou not said that whatsoe'er is done
Unto Thy weakest and Thy humblest one
Is even done to Thee?
In that sad victim, then,
Child of Thy pitying love, I see Thee stand;
Once more the jest-word of a mocking band,
Bound, sold, and scourged again!
A Christian up for sale!
Wet with her blood your whips, o'ertask her frame,
Make her life loathsome with your wrong and shame,
Her patience shall not fail!
A heathen hand might deal
Back on your heads the gathered wrong of years:
But her low, broken prayer and nightly tears,
Ye neither heed nor feel.
Con well thy lesson o'er,
Thou prudent teacher, tell the toiling slave
No dangerous tale of Him who came to save
The outcast and the poor.
But wisely shut the ray
Of God's free Gospel from her simple heart,
And to her darkened mind alone impart
One stern command, Obey!
So shalt thou deftly raise
The market price of human flesh; and while
On thee, their pampered guest, the planters smile,
Thy church shall praise.
Grave, reverend men shall tell
From Northern pulpits how thy work was blest,

While in that vile South Sodom first and best,
Thy poor disciples. sell.
Oh, shame! the Moslem thrall,
Who, with his master, to the Prophet kneels,
While turning to the sacred Kebla feels
His fetters break and fall.
Cheers for the turbaned Bey
Of robber-peopled Tunis! he hath torn
The dark slave-dungeons open, and hath borne
Their inmates into day:
But our poor slave in vain.
Turns to the Christian shrine his aching eyes;
Its rites will only swell his market price,
And rivet on his chain.
God of all right! how long
Shall priestly robbers at Thine altar stand,
Lifting in prayer to Thee, the bloody hand
And haughty brow of wrong?
Oh, from the fields of cane,
From the low rice-swamp, from the trader's cell;
From the black slave-ship's foul and loathsome hell,
And coffle's weary chain;
Hoarse, horrible, and strong,
Rises to Heaven that agonizing cry,
Filling the arches of the hollow sky,
How long, O God, how long?

The Crisis

Across the Stony Mountains, o'er the desert's drouth and sand,
The circles of our empire touch the western ocean's strand;
From slumberous Timpanogos, to Gila, wild and free,
Flowing down from Nuevo-Leon to California's sea;
And from the mountains of the east, to Santa Rosa's shore,
The eagles of Mexitli shall beat the air no more.
O Vale of Rio Bravo! Let thy simple children weep;
Close watch about their holy fire let maids of Pecos keep;
Let Taos send her cry across Sierra Madre's pines,
And Santa Barbara toll her bells amidst her corn and vines;
For lo! the pale land-seekers come, with eager eyes of gain,
Wide scattering, like the bison herds on broad Salada's plain.
Let Sacramento's herdsmen heed what sound the winds bring down
Of footsteps on the crisping snow, from cold Nevada's crown!
Full hot and fast the Saxon rides, with rein of travel slack,
And, bending o'er his saddle, leaves the sunrise at his back;
By many a lonely river, and gorge of fir and pine,
On many a wintry hill-top, his nightly camp-fires shine.
O countrymen and brothers! that land of lake and plain,
Of salt wastes alternating with valleys fat with grain;
Of mountains white with winter, looking downward, cold, serene,
On their feet with spring-vines tangled and lapped in softest green;
Swift through whose black volcanic gates, o'er many a sunny vale,

Wind-like the Arapahoe sweeps the bison's dusty trail!
Great spaces yet untravelled, great lakes whose mystic shores
The Saxon rifle never heard, nor dip of Saxon oars;
Great herds that wander all unwatched, wild steeds that none have tamed,
Strange fish in unknown streams, and birds the Saxon never named;
Deep mines, dark mountain crucibles, where Nature's chemic powers
Work out the Great Designer's will; all these ye say are ours!
Forever ours! for good or ill, on us the burden lies;
God's balance, watched by angels, is hung across the skies.
Shall Justice, Truth, and Freedom turn the poised and trembling scale?
Or shall the Evil triumph, and robber Wrong prevail?
Shall the broad land o'er which our flag in starry splendor waves,
Forego through us its freedom, and bear the tread of slaves?
The day is breaking in the East of which the prophets told,
And brightens up the sky of Time the Christian Age of Gold;
Old Might to Right is yielding, battle blade to clerkly pen,
Earth's monarchs are her peoples, and her serfs stand up as men;
The isles rejoice together, in a day are nations born,
And the slave walks free in Tunis, and by Stamboul's Golden Horn!
Is this, O countrymen of mine! a day for us to sow
The soil of new-gained empire with slavery's seeds of woe?
To feed with our fresh life-blood the Old World's cast-off crime,
Dropped, like some monstrous early birth, from the tired lap of Time?
To run anew the evil race the old lost nations ran,
And die like them of unbelief of God, and wrong of man?
Great Heaven! Is this our mission? End in this the prayers and tears,
The toil, the strife, the watchings of our younger, better years?
Still as the Old World rolls in light, shall ours in shadow turn,
A beamless Chaos, cursed of God, through outer darkness borne?
Where the far nations looked for light, a blackness in the air?
Where for words of hope they listened, the long wail of despair?
The Crisis presses on us; face to face with us it stands,
With solemn lips of question, like the Sphinx in Egypt's sands!
This day we fashion Destiny, our web of Fate we spin;
This day for all hereafter choose we holiness or sin,
Even now from starry Gerizim, or Ebal's cloudy crown
We call the dews of blessing or the bolts of cursing down!
By all for which the martyrs bore their agony and shame;
By all the warning words of truth with which the prophets came;
By the Future which awaits us; by all the hopes which cast
Their faint and trembling beams across the blackness of the Past;
And by the blessed thought of Him who for Earth's freedom died,
O my people! O my brothers! let us choose the righteous side.
So shall the Northern pioneer go joyful on his way;
To wed Penobscot's waters to San Francisco's bay;
To make the rugged places smooth, and sow the vales with grain;
And bear, with Liberty and Law, the Bible in his train:
The mighty West shall bless the East, and sea shall answer sea,
And mountain unto mountain call, Praise God for we are free!

The Curse Of The Charter-Breakers

In Westminster's royal halls,
Robed in their pontificals,
England's ancient prelates stood
For the people's right and good.
Closed around the waiting crowd,
Dark and still, like winter's cloud;
King and council, lord and knight,
Squire and yeoman, stood in sight;
Stood to hear the priest rehearse,
In God's name, the Church's curse,
By the tapers round them lit,
Slowly, sternly uttering it.
'Right of voice in framing laws,
Right of peers to try each cause;
Peasant homestead, mean and small,
Sacred as the monarch's hall,
'Whoso lays his hand on these,
England's ancient liberties;
Whoso breaks, by word or deed,
England's vow at Runnymede;
'Be he Prince or belted knight,
Whatsoe'er his rank or might,
If the highest, then the worst,
Let him live and die accursed.
'Thou, who to Thy Church hast given
Keys alike, of hell and heaven,
Make our word and witness sure,
Let the curse we speak endure!'
Silent, while that curse was said,
Every bare and listening head
Bowed in reverent awe, and then
All the people said, Amen!
Seven times the bells have tolled,
For the centuries gray and old,
Since that stoled and mitred band
Cursed the tyrants of their land.
Since the priesthood, like a tower,
Stood between the poor and power;
And the wronged and trodden down
Blessed the abbot's shaven crown.
Gone, thank God, their wizard spell,
Lost, their keys of heaven and hell;
Yet I sigh for men as bold
As those bearded priests of old.
Now, too oft the priesthood wait
At the threshold of the state;
Waiting for the beck and nod
Of its power as law and God.
Fraud exults, while solemn words
Sanctify his stolen hoards;
Slavery laughs, while ghostly lips
Bless his manacles and whips.

Not on them the poor rely,
Not to them looks liberty,
Who with fawning falsehood cower
To the wrong, when clothed with power.
Oh, to see them meanly cling,
Round the master, round the king,
Sported with, and sold and bought,
Pitifuller sight is not!
Tell me not that this must be:
God's true priest is always free;
Free, the needed truth to speak,
Right the wronged, and raise the weak.
Not to fawn on wealth and state,
Leaving Lazarus at the gate;
Not to peddle creeds like wares;
Got to mutter hireling prayers;
Nor to paint the new life's bliss
On the sable ground of this;
Golden streets for idle knave,
Sabbath rest for weary slave!
Not for words and works like these,
Priest of God, thy mission is;
But to make earth's desert glad,
In its Eden greenness clad;
And to level manhood bring
Lord and peasant, serf and king;
And the Christ of God to find
In the humblest of thy kind!.
Thine to work as well as pray,
Clearing thorny wrongs away;
Plucking up the weeds of sin,
Letting heaven's warm sunshine in;
Watching on the hills of Faith.;
Listening what the spirit saith,
Of the dim-seen light afar,
Growing like a nearing star.
God's interpreter art thou,
To the waiting ones below;
'Twixt them and its light midway
Heralding the better day;
Catching gleams of temple spires,
Hearing notes of angel choirs,
Where, as yet unseen of them,
Comes the New Jerusalem!
Like the seer of Patmos gazing,
On the glory downward blazing;
Till upon Earth's grateful sod
Rests the City of our God!

The Emancipation Group
Amidst thy sacred effigies

Of old renown give place,
O city, Freedom-loved! to his
Whose hand unchained a race.
Take the worn frame, that rested not
Save in a martyr's grave;
The care-lined face, that none forgot,
Bent to the kneeling slave.
Let man be free! The mighty word
He spake was not his own;
An impulse from the Highest stirred
These chiselled lips alone.
The cloudy sign, the fiery guide,
Along his pathway ran,
And Nature, through his voice, denied
The ownership of man.
We rest in peace where these sad eyes
Saw peril, strife, and pain;
His was the nation's sacrifice,
And ours the priceless gain.
O symbol of God's will on earth
As it is done above!
Bear witness to the cost and worth
Of justice and of love.
Stand in thy place and testify
To coming ages long,
That truth is stronger than a lie,
And righteousness than wrong.

The Farewell
Of A Virginia Slave Mother To Her Daughters Sold Into Southern Bondage

Gone, gone, sold and gone
To the rice-swamp dank and lone.
Where the slave-whip ceaseless swings
Where the noisome insect stings
Where the fever demon strews
Poison with the falling dews
Where the sickly sunbeams glare
Through the hot and misty air;
Gone, gone, sold and gone,
To the rice-swamp dank and lone,
From Virginia's hills and waters;
Woe is me, my stolen daughters!

Gone, gone, sold and gone
To the rice-swamp dank and lone
There no mother's eye is near them,
There no mother's ear can hear them;
Never, when the torturing lash
Seams their back with many a gash
Shall a mother's kindness bless them
Or a mother's arms caress them.

Gone, gone, sold and gone,
To the rice-swamp dank and lone,
From Virginia's hills and waters;
Woe is me, my stolen daughters!

Gone, gone, sold and gone,
To the rice-swamp dank and lone,
Oh, when weary, sad, and slow,
From the fields at night they go
Faint with toil, and racked with pain
To their cheerless homes again,
There no brother's voice shall greet them
There no father's welcome meet them.
Gone, gone, sold and gone,
To the rice-swamp dank and lone,
From Virginia's hills and waters;
Woe is me, my stolen daughters!

Gone, gone, sold and gone,
To the rice-swamp dank and lone
From the tree whose shadow lay
On their childhood's place of play;
From the cool sprmg where they drank;
Rock, and hill, and rivulet bank;
From the solemn house of prayer,
And the holy counsels there;
Gone, gone, sold and gone,
To the rice-swamp dank and lone,
From Virginia's hills and waters;
Woe is me, my stolen daughters!

Gone, gone, sold and gone,
To the rice-swamp dank and lone;
Toiling through the weary day,
And at night the spoiler's prey.
Oh, that they had earlier died,
Sleeping calmly, side by side,
Where the tyrant's power is o'er
And the fetter galls no more!
Gone, gone, sold and gone,
To the rice-swamp dank and lone;
From Virginia's hills and waters
Woe is me, my stolen daughters!

Gone, gone, sold and gone,
To the rice-swamp dank and lone;
By the holy love He beareth;
By the bruised reed He spareth;
Oh, may He, to whom alone
All their cruel wrongs are known,
Still their hope and refuge prove,
With a more than mother's love.

Gone, gone, sold and gone,
To the rice-swamp dank and lone,
From Virginia's hills and waters;
Woe is me, my stolen daughters!

The Golden Wedding Of Longwood

With fifty years between you and your well-kept wedding vow,
The Golden Age, old friends of mine, is not a fable now.

And, sweet as has life's vintage been through all your pleasant past,
Still, as at Cana's marriage-feast, the best wine is the last!

Again before me, with your names, fair Chester's landscape comes,
Its meadows, woods, and ample barns, and quaint, stone-builded homes.

The smooth-shorn vales, the wheaten slopes, the boscage green and soft,
Of which their poet sings so well from towered Cedarcroft.

And lo! from all the country-side come neighbors, kith and kin;
From city, hamlet, farm-house old, the wedding guests come in.

And they who, without scrip or purse, mob-hunted, travel-worn,
In Freedom's age of martyrs came, as victors now return.

Older and slower, yet the same, files in the long array,
And hearts are light and eyes are glad, though heads are badger-gray.

The fire-tried men of Thirty-eight who saw with me the fall,
Midst roaring flames and shouting mob, of Pennsylvania Hall;

And they of Lancaster who turned the cheeks of tyrants pale,
Singing of freedom through the grates of Moyamensing jail!

And haply with them, all unseen, old comrades, gone before,
Pass, silently as shadows pass, within your open door,

The eagle face of Lindley Coates, brave Garrett's daring zeal,
Christian grace of Pennock, the steadfast heart of Neal.

Ah me! beyond all power to name, the worthies tried and true,
Grave men, fair women, youth and maid, pass by in hushed review.

Of varying faiths, a common cause fused all their hearts in one.
God give them now, whate'er their names, the peace of duty done!

How gladly would I tread again the old-remembered places,
Sit down beside your hearth once more and look in the dear old faces!

And thank you for the lessons your fifty years are teaching,
For honest lives that louder speak than half our noisy preaching;

For your steady faith and courage in that dark and evil time,
When the Golden Rule was treason, and to feed the hungry, crime;

For the poor slave's house of refuge when the hounds were on his track,
And saint and sinner, church and state, joined hands to send him back.

Blessings upon you! What you did for each sad, suffering one,
So homeless, faint, and naked, unto our Lord was done!

Fair fall on Kennett's pleasant vales and Longwood's bowery ways
The mellow sunset of your lives, friends of my early days.

May many more of quiet years be added to your sum,
And, late at last, in tenderest love, the beckoning angel come.

Dear hearts are here, dear hearts are there, alike below, above;
Our friends are now in either world, and love is sure of love.

The Legend of St. Mark

The day is closing dark and cold,
With roaring blast and sleety showers;
And through the dusk the lilacs wear
The bloom of snow, instead of flowers.

I turn me from the gloom without,
To ponder o'er a tale of old;
A legend of the age of Faith,
By dreaming monk or abbess told.

On Tintoretto's canvas lives
That fancy of a loving heart,
In graceful lines and shapes of power,
And hues immortal as his art.

In Provence (so the story runs)
There lived a lord, to whom, as slave,
A peasant-boy of tender years
The chance of trade or conquest gave.

Forth-looking from the castle tower,
Beyond the hills with almonds dark,
The straining eye could scarce discern
The chapel of the good St. Mark.

And there, when bitter word or fare
The service of the youth repaid,
By stealth, before that holy shrine,
For grace to bear his wrong, he prayed.

The steed stamped at the castle gate,
The boar-hunt sounded on the hill;

Why stayed the Baron from the chase,
With looks so stern, and words so ill?

'Go, bind yon slave! and let him learn,
By scath of fire and strain of cord,
How ill they speed who give dead saints
The homage due their living lord!'

They bound him on the fearful rack,
When, through the dungeon's vaulted dark,
He saw the light of shining robes,
And knew the face of good St. Mark.

Then sank the iron rack apart,
The cords released their cruel clasp,
The pincers, with their teeth of fire,
Fell broken from the torturer's grasp.

And lo! before the Youth and Saint,
Barred door and wall of stone gave way;
And up from bondage and the night
They passed to freedom and the day!

O dreaming monk! thy tale is true;
O painter! true thy pencil's art;
in tones of hope and prophecy,
Ye whisper to my listening heart!

Unheard no burdened heart's appeal
Moans up to God's inclining ear;
Unheeded by his tender eye,
Falls to the earth no sufferer's tear.

For still the Lord alone is God
The pomp and power of tyrant man
Are scattered at his lightest breath,
Like chaff before the winnower's fan.

Not always shall the slave uplift
His heavy hands to Heaven in vain.
God's angel, like the good St. Mark,
Comes shining down to break his chain!

O weary ones! ye may not see
Your helpers in their downward flight;
Nor hear the sound of silver wings
Slow beating through the hush of night!

But not the less gray Dothan shone,
With sunbright watchers bending low,
That Fear's dim eye beheld alone
The spear-heads of the Syrian foe.

There are, who, like the Seer of old,
Can see the helpers God has sent,
And how life's rugged mountain-side
Is white with many an angel tent!

They hear the heralds whom our Lord
Sends down his pathway to prepare;
And light, from others hidden, shines
On their high place of faith and prayer.

Let such, for earth's despairing ones,
Hopeless, yet longing to be free,
Breathe once again the Prophet's prayer
'Lord, ope their eyes, that they may see!'

The Lumbermen

Wildly round our woodland quarters
Sad-voiced Autumn grieves;
Thickly down these swelling waters
Float his fallen leaves.
Through the tall and naked timber,
Column-like and old,
Gleam the sunsets of November,
From their skies of gold.
O'er us, to the southland heading,
Screams the gray wild-goose;
On the night-frost sounds the treading
Of the brindled moose.
Noiseless creeping, while we're sleeping,
Frost his task-work plies;
Soon, his icy bridges heaping,
Shall our log-piles rise.
When, with sounds of smothered thunder,
On some night of rain,
Lake and river break asunder
Winter's weakened chain,
Down the wild March flood shall bear them
To the saw-mill's wheel,
Or where Steam, the slave, shall tear them
With his teeth of steel.
Be it starlight, be it moonlight,
In these vales below,
When the earliest beams of sunlight
Streak the mountain's snow,
Crisps the hoar-frost, keen and early,
To our hurrying feet,
And the forest echoes clearly
All our blows repeat.
Where the crystal Ambijejis
Stretches broad and clear,

And Millnoket's pine-black ridges
Hide the browsing deer:
Where, through lakes and wide morasses,
Or through rocky walls,
Swift and strong, Penobscot passes
White with foamy falls;
Where, through clouds, are glimpses given
Of Katahdin's sides,
Rock and forest piled to heaven,
Torn and ploughed by slides!
Far below, the Indian trapping,
In the sunshine warm;
Far above, the snow-cloud wrapping
Half the peak in storm!
Where are mossy carpets better
Than the Persian weaves,
And than Eastern perfumes sweeter
Seem the fading leaves;
And a music wild and solemn,
From the pine-tree's height,
Rolls its vast and sea-like volume
On the wind of night;
Make we here our camp of winter;
And, through sleet and snow,
Pitchy knot and beechen splinter
On our hearth shall glow.
Here, with mirth to lighten duty,
We shall lack alone
Woman's smile and girlhood's beauty,
Childhood's lisping tone.
But their hearth is brighter burning
For our toil to-day;
And the welcome of returning
Shall our loss repay,
When, like seamen from the waters,
From the woods we come,
Greeting sisters, wives, and daughters,
Angels of our home!
Not for us the measured ringing
From the village spire,
Not for us the Sabbath singing
Of the sweet-voiced choir.
Ours the old, majestic temple,
Where God's brightness shines
Down the dome so grand and ample,
Propped by lofty pines!
Through each branch-enwoven skylight,
Speaks He in the breeze,
As of old beneath the twilight
Of lost Eden's trees!
For His ear, the inward feeling
Needs no outward tongue;

He can see the spirit kneeling
While the axe is swung.
Heeding truth alone, and turning
From the false and dim,
Lamp of toil or altar burning
Are alike to Him.
Strike, then, comrades! Trade is waiting
On our rugged toil;
Far ships waiting for the freighting
Of our woodland spoil!
Ships, whose traffic links these highlands,
Bleak and cold, of ours,
With the citron-planted islands
Of a clime of flowers;
To our frosts the tribute bringing
Of eternal heats;
In our lap of winter flinging
Tropic fruits and sweets.
Cheerly, on the axe of labor,
Let the sunbeams dance,
Better than the flash of sabre
Or the gleam of lance!
Strike! With every blow is given
Freer sun and sky,
And the long-hid earth to heaven
Looks, with wondering eye!
Loud behind us grow the murmurs
Of the age to come;
Clang of smiths, and tread of farmers,
Bearing harvest home!
Here her virgin lap with treasures
Shall the green earth fill;
Waving wheat and golden maize-ears
Crown each beechen hill.
Keep who will the city's alleys,
Take the smooth-shorn plain;
Give to us the cedarn valleys,
Rocks and hills of Maine!
In our North-land, wild and woody,
Let us still have part:
Rugged nurse and mother sturdy,
Hold us to thy heart!
Oh, our free hearts beat the warmer
For thy breath of snow;
And our tread is all the firmer
For thy rocks below.
Freedom, hand in hand with labor,
Walketh strong and brave;
On the forehead of his neighbor
No man writeth Slave!
Lo, the day breaks! old Katahdin's
Pine-trees show its fires,

While from these dim forest gardens
Rise their blackened spires.
Up, my comrades! up and doing!
Manhood's rugged play
Still renewing, bravely hewing
Through the world our way!

A Legend Of The Mantle Of St. John De Matha
A strong and mighty Angel,
Calm, terrible, and bright,
The cross in blended red and blue
Upon his mantle white!
Two captives by him kneeling,
Each on his broken chain,
Sang praise to God who raiseth
The dead to life again!
Dropping his cross-wrought mantle,
'Wear this,' the Angel said;
'Take thou, O Freedom's priest, its sign,
The white, the blue, and red.'
Then rose up John de Matha
In the strength the Lord Christ gave,
And begged through all the land of France
The ransom of the slave.
The gates of tower and castle
Before him open flew,
The drawbridge at his coming fell,
The door-bolt backward drew.
For all men owned his errand,
And paid his righteous tax;
And the hearts of lord and peasant
Were in his hands as wax.
At last, outbound from Tunis,
His bark her anchor weighed,
Freighted with seven-score Christian souls
Whose ransom he had paid.
But, torn by Paynim hatred,
Her sails in tatters hung;
And on the wild waves, rudderless,
A shattered hulk she swung.
'God save us!' cried the captain,
'For naught can man avail;
Oh, woe betide the ship that lacks
Her rudder and her sail!
'Behind us are the Moormen;
At sea we sink or strand:
There's death upon the water,
There's death upon the land!'
Then up spake John de Matha:
'God's errands never fail!
Take thou the mantle which I wear,

And make of it a sail.'
They raised the cross-wrought mantle,
The blue, the white, the red;
And straight before the wind off-shore
The ship of Freedom sped.
'God help us!' cried the seamen,
'For vain is mortal skill:
The good ship on a stormy sea
Is drifting at its will.'
Then up spake John de Matha:
'My mariners, never fear!
The Lord whose breath has filled her sail
May well our vessel steer!'
So on through storm and darkness
They drove for weary hours;
And lo! the third gray morning shone
On Ostia's friendly towers.
And on the walls the watchers
The ship of mercy knew,
They knew far off its holy cross,
The red, the white, and blue.
And the bells in all the steeples
Rang out in glad accord,
To welcome home to Christian soil
The ransomed of the Lord.
So runs the ancient legend
By bard and painter told;
And lo! the cycle rounds again,
The new is as the old!
With rudder foully broken,
And sails by traitors torn,
Our country on a midnight sea
Is waiting for the morn.
Before her, nameless terror;
Behind, the pirate foe;
The clouds are black above her,
The sea is white below.
The hope of all who suffer,
The dread of all who wrong,
She drifts in darkness and in storm,
How long, O Lord! how long?
But courage, O my mariners!
Ye shall not suffer wreck,
While up to God the freedman's prayers
Are rising from your deck.
Is not your sail the banner
Which God hath blest anew,
The mantle that De Matha wore,
The red, the white, the blue?
Its hues are all of heaven,
The red of sunset's dye,
The whiteness of the moon-lit cloud,

The blue of morning's sky.
Wait cheerily, then, O mariners,
For daylight and for land;
The breath of God is in your sail,
Your rudder is His hand.
Sail on, sail on, deep-freighted
With blessings and with hopes;
The saints of old with shadowy hands
Are pulling at your ropes.
Behind ye holy martyrs
Uplift the palm and crown;
Before ye unborn ages send
Their benedictions down.
Take heart from John de Matha!
God's errands never fail!
Sweep on through storm and darkness,
The thunder and the hail!
Sail on! The morning cometh,
The port ye yet shall win;
And all the bells of God shall ring
The good ship bravely in!

The Merrimac

Stream of my fathers! sweetly still
The sunset rays thy valley fill;
Poured slantwise down the long defile,
Wave, wood, and spire beneath them smile.
I see the winding Powow fold
The green hill in its belt of gold,
And following down its wavy line,
Its sparkling waters blend with thine.
There 's not a tree upon thy side,
Nor rock, which thy returning tide
As yet hath left abrupt and stark
Above thy evening water-mark;
No calm cove with its rocky hem,
No isle whose emerald swells begin
Thy broad, smooth current; not a sail
Bowed to the freshening ocean gale;
No small boat with its busy oars,
Nor gray wall sloping to thy shores;
Nor farm-house with its maple shade,
Or rigid poplar colonnade,
But lies distinct and full in sight,
Beneath this gush of sunset light.
Centuries ago, that harbor-bar,
Stretching its length of foam afar,
And Salisbury's beach of shining sand,
And yonder island's wave-smoothed strand,
Saw the adventurer's tiny sail,
Flit, stooping from the eastern gale;

And o'er these woods and waters broke
The cheer from Britain's hearts of oak,
As brightly on the voyager's eye,
Weary of forest, sea, and sky,
Breaking the dull continuous wood,
The Merrimac rolled down his flood;
Mingling that clear pellucid brook,
Which channels vast Agioochook
When spring-time's sun and shower unlock
The frozen fountains of the rock,
And more abundant waters given
From that pure lake, 'The Smile of Heaven,'
Tributes from vale and mountain-side,
With ocean's dark, eternal tide!

On yonder rocky cape, which braves
The stormy challenge of the waves,
Midst tangled vine and dwarfish wood,
The hardy Anglo-Saxon stood,
Planting upon the topmost crag
The staff of England's battle-flag;
And, while from out its heavy fold
Saint George's crimson cross unrolled,
Midst roll of drum and trumpet blare,
And weapons brandishing in air,
He gave to that lone promontory
The sweetest name in all his story;
Of her, the flower of Islam's daughters,
Whose harems look on Stamboul's waters,
Who, when the chance of war had bound
The Moslem chain his limbs around,
Wreathed o'er with silk that iron chain,
Soothed with her smiles his hours of pain,
And fondly to her youthful slave
A dearer gift than freedom gave.

But look! the yellow light no more
Streams down on wave and verdant shore;
And clearly on the calm air swells
The twilight voice of distant bells.
From Ocean's bosom, white and thin,
The mists come slowly rolling in;
Hills, woods, the river's rocky rim,
Amidst the sea-like vapor swim,
While yonder lonely coast-light, set
Within its wave-washed minaret,
Half quenched, a beamless star and pale,
Shines dimly through its cloudy veil!

Home of my fathers!-I have stood
Where Hudson rolled his lordly flood
Seen sunrise rest and sunset fade

Along his frowning Palisade;
Looked down the Appalachian peak
On Juniata's silver streak;
Have seen along his valley gleam
The Mohawk's softly winding stream;
The level light of sunset shine
Through broad Potomac's hem of pine;
And autumn's rainbow-tinted banner
Hang lightly o'er the Susquehanna;
Yet wheresoe'er his step might be,
Thy wandering child looked back to thee!
Heard in his dreams thy river's sound
Of murmuring on its pebbly bound,
The unforgotten swell and roar
Of waves on thy familiar shore;
And saw, amidst the curtained gloom
And quiet of his lonely room,
Thy sunset scenes before him pass;
As, in Agrippa's magic glass,
The loved and lost arose to view,
Remembered groves in greenness grew,
Bathed still in childhood's morning dew,
Along whose bowers of beauty swept
Whatever Memory's mourners wept,
Sweet faces, which the charnel kept,
Young, gentle eyes, which long had slept;
And while the gazer leaned to trace,
More near, some dear familiar face,
He wept to find the vision flown,
A phantom and a dream alone!

The New Wife And The Old

Dark the halls, and cold the feast,
Gone the bridemaids, gone the priest.
All is over, all is done,
Twain of yesterday are one!
Blooming girl and manhood gray,
Autumn in the arms of May!

Hushed within and hushed without,
Dancing feet and wrestlers' shout;
Dies the bonfire on the hill;
All is dark and all is still,
Save the starlight, save the breeze
Moaning through the graveyard trees,
And the great sea-waves below,
Pulse of the midnight beating slow.

From the brief dream of a bride
She hath wakened, at his side.
With half-uttered shriek and start,

Feels she not his beating heart?
And the pressure of his arm,
And his breathing near and warm?

Lightly from the bridal bed
Springs that fair dishevelled head,
And a feeling, new, intense,
Half of shame, half innocence,
Maiden fear and wonder speaks
Through her lips and changing cheeks.

From the oaken mantel glowing,
Faintest light the lamp is throwing
On the mirror's antique mould,
High-backed chair, and wainscot old,
And, through faded curtains stealing,
His dark sleeping face revealing.

Listless lies the strong man there,
Silver-streaked his careless hair;
Lips of love have left no trace
On that hard and haughty face;
And that forehead's knitted thought
Love's soft hand hath not unwrought.

'Yet,' she sighs, 'he loves me well,
More than these calm lips will tell.
Stooping to my lowly state,
He hath made me rich and great,
And I bless him, though he be
Hard and stern to all save me!'

While she speaketh, falls the light
O'er her fingers small and white;
Gold and gem, and costly ring
Back the timid lustre fling,-
Love's selectest gifts, and rare,
His proud hand had fastened there.

Gratefully she marks the glow
From those tapering lines of snow;
Fondly o'er the sleeper bending
His black hair with golden blending,
In her soft and light caress,
Cheek and lip together press.

Ha!-that start of horror! why
That wild stare and wilder cry,
Full of terror, full of pain?
Is there madness in her brain?
Hark! that gasping, hoarse and low,
'Spare me,-spare me,-let me go!'

God have mercy!-icy cold
Spectral hands her own enfold,
Drawing silently from them
Love's fair gifts of gold and gem.
'Waken! save me!' still as death
At her side he slumbereth.

Ring and bracelet all are gone,
And that ice-cold hand withdrawn;
But she hears a murmur low,
Full of sweetness, full of woe,
Half a sigh and half a moan
'Fear not! give the dead her own!'

Ah!-the dead wife's voice she knows!
That cold hand whose pressure froze,
Once in warmest life had borne
Gem and band her own hath worn.
'Wake thee! wake thee!' Lo, his eyes
Open with a dull surprise.

In his arms the strong man folds her,
Closer to his breast he holds her;
Trembling limbs his own are meeting,
And he feels her heart's quick beating
'Nay, my dearest, why this fear?'
'Hush!' she saith, 'the dead is here!'

'Nay, a dream,-an idle dream.'
But before the lamp's pale gleam
Tremblingly her hand she raises.
There no more the diamond blazes,
Clasp of pearl, or ring of gold,
'Ah!' she sighs, 'her hand was cold!'

Broken words of cheer he saith,
But his dark lip quivereth,
And as o'er the past he thinketh,
From his young wife's arms he shrinketh;
Can those soft arms round him lie,
Underneath his dead wife's eye?

She her fair young head can rest
Soothed and childlike on his breast,
And in trustful innocence
Draw new strength and courage thence;
He, the proud man, feels within
But the cowardice of sin!

She can murmur in her thought
Simple prayers her mother taught,

And His blessed angels call,
Whose great love is over all;
He, alone, in prayerless pride,
Meets the dark Past at her side!

One, who living shrank with dread
From his look, or word, or tread,
Unto whom her early grave
Was as freedom to the slave,
Moves him at this midnight hour,
With the dead's unconscious power!

Ah, the dead, the unforgot!
From their solemn homes of thought,
Where the cypress shadows blend
Darkly over foe and friend,
Or in love or sad rebuke,
Back upon the living look.

And the tenderest ones and weakest,
Who their wrongs have borne the meekest,
Lifting from those dark, still places,
Sweet and sad-remembered faces,
O'er the guilty hearts behind
An unwitting triumph find.

The New Year

The wave is breaking on the shore,
The echo fading from the chime;
Again the shadow moveth o'er
The dial-plate of time!
O seer-seen Angel! waiting now
With weary feet on sea and shore,
Impatient for the last dread vow
That time shall be no more!
Once more across thy sleepless eye
The semblance of a smile has passed:
The year departing leaves more nigh
Time's fearfullest and last.
Oh, in that dying year hath been
The sum of all since time began;
The birth and death, the joy and pain,
Of Nature and of Man.
Spring, with her change of sun and shower,
And streams released from Winter's chain,
And bursting bud, and opening flower,
And greenly growing grain;
And Summer's shade, and sunshine warm,
And rainbows o'er her hill-tops bowed,
And voices in her rising storm;
God speaking from His cloud!

And Autumn's fruits and clustering sheaves,
And soft, warm days of golden light,
The glory of her forest leaves,
And harvest-moon at night;
And Winter with her leafless grove,
And prisoned stream, and drifting snow,
The brilliance of her heaven above
And of her earth below:
And man, in whom an angel's mind
With earth's low instincts finds abode,
The highest of the links which bind
Brute nature to her God;
His infant eye hath seen the light,
His childhood's merriest laughter rung,
And active sports to manlier might
The nerves of boyhood strung!
And quiet love, and passion's fires,
Have soothed or burned in manhood's breast,
And lofty aims and low desires
By turns disturbed his rest.
The wailing of the newly-born
Has mingled with the funeral knell;
And o'er the dying's ear has gone
The merry marriage-bell.
And Wealth has filled his halls with mirth,
While Want, in many a humble shed,
Toiled, shivering by her cheerless hearth,
The live-long night for bread.
And worse than all, the human slave,
The sport of lust, and pride, and scorn!
Plucked off the crown his Maker gave,
His regal manhood gone!
Oh, still,my country! o'er thy plains,
Blackened with slavery's blight and ban,
That human chattel drags his chains,
An uncreated man!
And still, where'er to sun and breeze,
My country, is thy flag unrolled,
With scorn, the gazing stranger sees
A stain on every fold.
Oh, tear the gorgeous emblem down!
It gathers scorn from every eye,
And despots smile and good men frown
Whene'er it passes by.
Shame! shame! its starry splendors glow
Above the slaver's loathsome jail;
Its folds are ruffling even now
His crimson flag of sale.
Still round our country's proudest hall
The trade in human flesh is driven,
And at each careless hammer-fall
A human heart is riven.

And this, too, sanctioned by the men
Vested with power to shield the right,
And throw each vile and robber den
Wide open to the light.
Yet, shame upon them! there they sit,
Men of the North, subdued and still;
Meek, pliant poltroons, only fit
To work a master's will.
Sold, bargained off for Southern votes,
A passive herd of Northern mules,
Just braying through their purchased throats
Whate'er their owner rules.
And he,the basest of the base
The vilest of the vile, whose name,
Embalmed in infinite disgrace,
Is deathless in its shame!
A tool, to bolt the people's door
Against the people clamoring there,
An ass, to trample on their floor
A people's right of prayer!
Nailed to his self-made gibbet fast,
Self-pilloried to the public view,
A mark for every passing blast
Of scorn to whistle through;
There let him hang, and hear the boast
Of Southrons o'er their pliant tool,
A new Stylites on his post,
'Sacred to ridicule!'
Look we at home! our noble hall,
To Freedom's holy purpose given,
Now rears its black and ruined wall,
Beneath the wintry heaven,
Telling the story of its doom,
The fiendish mob, the prostrate law,
The fiery jet through midnight's gloom,
Our gazing thousands saw.
Look to our State! the poor man's right
Torn from him: and the sons of those
Whose blood in Freedom's sternest fight
Sprinkled the Jersey snows,
Outlawed within the land of Penn,
That Slavery's guilty fears might cease,
And those whom God created men
Toil on as brutes in peace.
Yet o'er the blackness of the storm
A bow of promise bends on high,
And gleams of sunshine, soft and warm,
Break through our clouded sky.
East, West, and North, the shout is heard,
Of freemen rising for the right:
Each valley hath its rallying word,
Each hill its signal light.

O'er Massachusetts' rocks of gray,
The strengthening light of freedom shines,
Rhode Island's Narragansett Bay,
And Vermont's snow-hung pines!
From Hudson's frowning palisades
To Alleghany's laurelled crest,
O'er lakes and prairies, streams and glades,
It shines upon the West.
Speed on the light to those who dwell
In Slavery's land of woe and sin,
And through the blackness of that hell,
Let Heaven's own light break in.
So shall the Southern conscience quake
Before that light poured full and strong,
So shall the Southern heart awake
To all the bondman's wrong.
And from that rich and sunny land
The song of grateful millions rise,
Like that of Israel's ransomed band
Beneath Arabians skies:
And all who now are bound beneath
Our banner's shade, our eagle's wing,
From Slavery's night of moral death
To light and life shall spring.
Broken the bondman's chain, and gone
The master's guilt, and hate, and fear,
And unto both alike shall dawn
A New and Happy Year.

The Peace Autumn
Thank God for rest, where none molest,
And none can make afraid;
For Peace that sits as Plenty's guest
Beneath the homestead shade!
Bring pike and gun, the sword's red scourge,
The negro's broken chains,
And beat them at the blacksmith's forge
To ploughshares for our plains.
Alike henceforth our hills of snow,
And vales where cotton flowers;
All streams that flow, all winds that blow,
Are Freedom's motive-powers.
Henceforth to Labor's chivalry
Be knightly honors paid;
For nobler than the sword's shall be
The sickle's accolade.
Build up an altar to the Lord,
O grateful hearts of ours!
And shape it of the greenest sward
That ever drank the showers.
Lay all the bloom of gardens there,

And there the orchard fruits;
Bring golden grain from sun and air,
From earth her goodly roots.
There let our banners droop and flow,
The stars uprise and fall;
Our roll of martyrs, sad and slow,
Let sighing breezes call.
Their names let hands of horn and tan
And rough-shod feet applaud,
Who died to make the slave a man,
And link with toil reward.
There let the common heart keep time
To such an anthem sung
As never swelled on poet's rhyme,
Or thrilled on singer's tongue.
Song of our burden and relief,
Of peace and long annoy;
The passion of our mighty grief
And our exceeding joy!
A song of praise to Him who filled
The harvests sown in years,
And gave each field a double yield
To feed our battle-years!
A song of faith that trusts the end
To match the good begun,
Nor doubts the power of Love to blend
The hearts of men as one!

The Pennsylvania Pilgrim
Prelude
I sing the Pilgrim of a softer clime
And milder speech than those brave men's who brought
To the ice and iron of our winter time
A will as firm, a creed as stern, and wrought
With one mailed hand, and with the other fought.
Simply, as fits my theme, in homely rhyme
I sing the blue-eyed German Spener taught,
Through whose veiled, mystic faith the Inward Light,
Steady and still, an easy brightness, shone,
Transfiguring all things in its radiance white.
The garland which his meekness never sought
I bring him; over fields of harvest sown
With seeds of blessing, now to ripeness grown,
I bid the sower pass before the reapers' sight.

The Pennsylvania Pilgrim
Never in tenderer quiet lapsed the day
From Pennsylvania's vales of spring away,
Where, forest-walled, the scattered hamlets lay

Along the wedded rivers. One long bar

Of purple cloud, on which the evening star
Shone like a jewel on a scimitar,

Held the sky's golden gateway. Through the deep
Hush of the woods a murmur seemed to creep,
The Schuylkill whispering in a voice of sleep.

All else was still. The oxen from their ploughs
Rested at last, and from their long day's browse
Came the dun files of Krisheim's home-bound cows.

And the young city, round whose virgin zone
The rivers like two mighty arms were thrown,
Marked by the smoke of evening fires alone,

Lay in the distance, lovely even then
With its fair women and its stately men
Gracing the forest court of William Penn,

Urban yet sylvan; in its rough-hewn frames
Of oak and pine the dryads held their claims,
And lent its streets their pleasant woodland names.

Anna Pastorius down the leafy lane
Looked city-ward, then stooped to prune again
Her vines and simples, with a sigh of pain.

For fast the streaks of ruddy sunset paled
In the oak clearing, and, as daylight failed,
Slow, overhead, the dusky night-birds sailed.

Again she looked: between green walls of shade,
With low-bent head as if with sorrow weighed,
Daniel Pastorius slowly came and said,

'God's peace be with thee, Anna!' Then he stood
Silent before her, wrestling with the mood
Of one who sees the evil and not good.

'What is it, my Pastorius?' As she spoke,
A slow, faint smile across his features broke,
Sadder than tears. 'Dear heart,' he said, 'our folk

'Are even as others. Yea, our goodliest Friends
Are frail; our elders have their selfish ends,
And few dare trust the Lord to make amends

'For duty's loss. So even our feeble word
For the dumb slaves the startled meeting heard
As if a stone its quiet waters stirred;

'And, as the clerk ceased reading, there began

A ripple of dissent which downward ran
In widening circles, as from man to man.

'Somewhat was said of running before sent,
Of tender fear that some their guide outwent,
Troublers of Israel. I was scarce intent

'On hearing, for behind the reverend row
Of gallery Friends, in dumb and piteous show,
I saw, methought, dark faces full of woe.

'And, in the spirit, I was taken where
They toiled and suffered; I was made aware
Of shame and wrath and anguish and despair!

'And while the meeting smothered our poor plea
With cautious phrase, a Voice there seemed to be,
As ye have done to these ye do to me!'

'So it all passed; and the old tithe went on
Of anise, mint, and cumin, till the sun
Set, leaving still the weightier work undone.

'Help, for the good man faileth! Who is strong,
If these be weak? Who shall rebuke the wrong,
If these consent? How long, O Lord! how long!'

He ceased; and, bound in spirit with the bound,
With folded arms, and eyes that sought the ground,
Walked musingly his little garden round.

About him, beaded with the falling dew,
Rare plants of power and herbs of healing grew,
Such as Van Helmont and Agrippa knew.

For, by the lore of Gorlitz' gentle sage,
With the mild mystics of his dreamy age
He read the herbal signs of nature's page,

As once he heard in sweet Von Merlau's' bowers
Fair as herself, in boyhood's happy hours,
The pious Spener read his creed in flowers.

'The dear Lord give us patience!' said his wife,
Touching with finger-tip an aloe, rife
With leaves sharp-pointed like an Aztec knife

Or Carib spear, a gift to William Penn
From the rare gardens of John Evelyn,
Brought from the Spanish Main by merchantmen.

'See this strange plant its steady purpose hold,

And, year by year, its patient leaves unfold,
Till the young eyes that watched it first are old.

'But some time, thou hast told me, there shall come
A sudden beauty, brightness, and perfume,
The century-moulded bud shall burst in bloom.

'So may the seed which hath been sown to-day
Grow with the years, and, after long delay,
Break into bloom, and God's eternal Yea!

'Answer at last the patient prayers of them
Who now, by faith alone, behold its stem
Crowned with the flowers of Freedom's diadem.

'Meanwhile, to feel and suffer, work and wait,
Remains for us. The wrong indeed is great,
But love and patience conquer soon or late.'

'Well hast thou said, my Anna!' Tenderer
Than youth's caress upon the head of her
Pastorius laid his hand. 'Shall we demur

'Because the vision tarrieth? In an hour
We dream not of, the slow-grown bud may flower,
And what was sown in weakness rise in power!'

Then through the vine-draped door whose legend read,
'Procul este profani!' Anna led
To where their child upon his little bed

Looked up and smiled. 'Dear heart,' she said, 'if we
Must bearers of a heavy burden be,
Our boy, God willing, yet the day shall see

'When from the gallery to the farthest seat,
Slave and slave-owner shall no longer meet,
But all sit equal at the Master's feet.'

On the stone hearth the blazing walnut block
Set the low walls a-glimmer, showed the cock
Rebuking Peter on the Van Wyck clock,

Shone on old tomes of law and physic, side
By side with Fox and Belimen, played at hide
And seek with Anna, midst her household pride

Of flaxen webs, and on the table, bare
Of costly cloth or silver cup, but where,
Tasting the fat shads of the Delaware,

The courtly Penn had praised the goodwife's cheer,

And quoted Horace o'er her home brewed beer,
Till even grave Pastorius smiled to hear.

In such a home, beside the Schuylkill's wave,
He dwelt in peace with God and man, and gave
Food to the poor and shelter to the slave.

For all too soon the New World's scandal shamed
The righteous code by Penn and Sidney framed,
And men withheld the human rights they claimed.

And slowly wealth and station sanction lent,
And hardened avarice, on its gains intent,
Stifled the inward whisper of dissent.

Yet all the while the burden rested sore
On tender hearts. At last Pastorius bore
Their warning message to the Church's door

In God's name; and the leaven of the word
Wrought ever after in the souls who heard,
And a dead conscience in its grave-clothes stirred

To troubled life, and urged the vain excuse
Of Hebrew custom, patriarchal use,
Good in itself if evil in abuse.

Gravely Pastorius listened, not the less
Discerning through the decent fig-leaf dress
Of the poor plea its shame of selfishness.

One Scripture rule, at least, was unforgot;
He hid the outcast, and betrayed him not;
And, when his prey the human hunter sought,

He scrupled not, while Anna's wise delay
And proffered cheer prolonged the master's stay,
To speed the black guest safely on his way.

Yet, who shall guess his bitter grief who lends
His life to some great cause, and finds his friends
Shame or betray it for their private ends?

How felt the Master when his chosen strove
In childish folly for their seats above;
And that fond mother, blinded by her love,

Besought him that her sons, beside his throne,
Might sit on either hand? Amidst his own
A stranger oft, companionless and lone,

God's priest and prophet stands. The martyr's pain

Is not alone from scourge and cell and chain;
Sharper the pang when, shouting in his train,

His weak disciples by their lives deny
The loud hosannas of their daily cry,
And make their echo of his truth a lie.

His forest home no hermit's cell he found,
Guests, motley-minded, drew his hearth around,
And held armed truce upon its neutral ground.

There Indian chiefs with battle-bows unstrung,
Strong, hero-limbed, like those whom Homer sung,
Pastorius fancied, when the world was young,

Came with their tawny women, lithe and tall,
Like bronzes in his friend Von Rodeck's hall,
Comely, if black, and not unpleasing all.

There hungry folk in homespun drab and gray
Drew round his board on Monthly Meeting day,
Genial, half merry in their friendly way.

Or, haply, pilgrims from the Fatherland,
Weak, timid, homesick, slow to understand
The New World's promise, sought his helping hand.

Or painful Kelpius from his hermit den
By Wissahickon, maddest of good men,
Dreamed o'er the Chiliast dreams of Petersen.

Deep in the woods, where the small river slid
Snake-like in shade, the Helmstadt Mystic hid,
Weird as a wizard, over arts forbid,

Reading the books of Daniel and of John,
And Behmen's Morning-Redness, through the Stone
Of Wisdom, vouchsafed to his eyes alone,

Whereby he read what man ne'er read before,
And saw the visions man shall see no more,
Till the great angel, striding sea and shore,

Shall bid all flesh await, on land or ships,
The warning trump of the Apocalypse,
Shattering the heavens before the dread eclipse.

Or meek-eyed Mennonist his bearded chin
Leaned o'er the gate; or Ranter, pure within,
Aired his perfection in a world of sin.

Or, talking of old home scenes, Op der Graaf

Teased the low back-log with his shodden staff,
Till the red embers broke into a laugh

And dance of flame, as if they fain would cheer
The rugged face, half tender, half austere,
Touched with the pathos of a homesick tear!

Or Sluyter, saintly familist, whose word
As law the Brethren of the Manor heard,
Announced the speedy terrors of the Lord,

And turned, like Lot at Sodom, from his race,
Above a wrecked world with complacent face
Riding secure upon his plank of grace!

Haply, from Finland's birchen groves exiled,
Manly in thought, in simple ways a child,
His white hair floating round his visage mild,

The Swedish pastor sought the Quaker's door,
Pleased from his neighbor's lips to hear once more
His long-disused and half-forgotten lore.

For both could baffle Babel's lingual curse,
And speak in Bion's Doric, and rehearse
Cleanthes' hymn or Virgil's sounding verse.

And oft Pastorius and the meek old man
Argued as Quaker and as Lutheran,
Ending in Christian love, as they began.

With lettered Lloyd on pleasant morns he strayed
Where Sommerhausen over vales of shade
Looked miles away, by every flower delayed,

Or song of bird, happy and free with one
Who loved, like him, to let his memory run
Over old fields of learning, and to sun

Himself in Plato's wise philosophies,
And dream with Philo over mysteries
Whereof the dreamer never finds the keys;

To touch all themes of thought, nor weakly stop
For doubt of truth, but let the buckets drop
Deep down and bring the hidden waters up

For there was freedom in that wakening time
Of tender souls; to differ was not crime;
The varying bells made up the perfect chime.

On lips unlike was laid the altar's coal,

The white, clear light, tradition-colored, stole
Through the stained oriel of each human soul.

Gathered from many sects, the Quaker brought
His old beliefs, adjusting to the thought
That moved his soul the creed his fathers taught.

One faith alone, so broad that all mankind
Within themselves its secret witness find,
The soul's communion with the Eternal Mind,

The Spirit's law, the Inward Rule and Guide,
Scholar and peasant, lord and serf, allied,
The polished Penn and Cromwell's Ironside.

As still in Hemskerck's Quaker Meeting, face
By face in Flemish detail, we may trace
How loose-mouthed boor and fine ancestral grace

Sat in close contrast,-the clipt-headed churl,
Broad market-dame, and simple serving-girl
By skirt of silk and periwig in curl

For soul touched soul; the spiritual treasure-trove
Made all men equal, none could rise above
Nor sink below that level of God's love.

So, with his rustic neighbors sitting down,
The homespun frock beside the scholar's gown,
Pastorius to the manners of the town

Added the freedom of the woods, and sought
The bookless wisdom by experience taught,
And learned to love his new-found home, while not

Forgetful of the old; the seasons went
Their rounds, and somewhat to his spirit lent
Of their own calm and measureless content.

Glad even to tears, he heard the robin sing
His song of welcome to the Western spring,
And bluebird borrowing from the sky his wing.

And when the miracle of autumn came,
And all the woods with many-colored flame
Of splendor, making summer's greenness lame,

Burned, unconsumed, a voice without a sound
Spake to him from each kindled bush around,
And made the strange, new landscape holy ground

And when the bitter north-wind, keen and swift,

Swept the white street and piled the dooryard drift,
He exercised, as Friends might say, his gift

Of verse, Dutch, English, Latin, like the hash
Of corn and beans in Indian succotash;
Dull, doubtless, but with here and there a flash

Of wit and fine conceit,-the good man's play
Of quiet fancies, meet to while away
The slow hours measuring off an idle day.

At evening, while his wife put on her look
Of love's endurance, from its niche he took
The written pages of his ponderous book.

And read, in half the languages of man,
His 'Rusca Apium,' which with bees began,
And through the gamut of creation ran.

Or, now and then, the missive of some friend
In gray Altorf or storied Nurnberg penned
Dropped in upon him like a guest to spend

The night beneath his roof-tree. Mystical
The fair Von Merlau spake as waters fall
And voices sound in dreams, and yet withal

Human and sweet, as if each far, low tone,
Over the roses of her gardens blown
Brought the warm sense of beauty all her own.

Wise Spener questioned what his friend could trace
Of spiritual influx or of saving grace
In the wild natures of the Indian race.

And learned Schurmberg, fain, at times, to look
From Talmud, Koran, Veds, and Pentateuch,
Sought out his pupil in his far-off nook,

To query with him of climatic change,
Of bird, beast, reptile, in his forest range,
Of flowers and fruits and simples new and strange.

And thus the Old and New World reached their hands
Across the water, and the friendly lands
Talked with each other from their severed strands.

Pastorius answered all: while seed and root
Sent from his new home grew to flower and fruit
Along the Rhine and at the Spessart's foot;

And, in return, the flowers his boyhood knew

Smiled at his door, the same in form and hue,
And on his vines the Rhenish clusters grew.

No idler he; whoever else might shirk,
He set his hand to every honest work,
Farmer and teacher, court and meeting clerk.

Still on the town seal his device is found,
Grapes, flax, and thread-spool on a trefoil ground,
With 'Vinum, Linum et Textrinum' wound.

One house sufficed for gospel and for law,
Where Paul and Grotius, Scripture text and saw,
Assured the good, and held the rest in awe.

Whatever legal maze he wandered through,
He kept the Sermon on the Mount in view,
And justice always into mercy grew.

No whipping-post he needed, stocks, nor jail,
Nor ducking-stool; the orchard-thief grew pale
At his rebuke, the vixen ceased to rail,

The usurer's grasp released the forfeit land;
The slanderer faltered at the witness-stand,
And all men took his counsel for command.

Was it caressing air, the brooding love
Of tenderer skies than German land knew of,
Green calm below, blue quietness above,

Still flow of water, deep repose of wood
That, with a sense of loving Fatherhood
And childlike trust in the Eternal Good,

Softened all hearts, and dulled the edge of hate,
Hushed strife, and taught impatient zeal to wait
The slow assurance of the better state?

Who knows what goadings in their sterner way
O'er jagged ice, relieved by granite gray,
Blew round the men of Massachusetts Bay?

What hate of heresy the east-wind woke?
What hints of pitiless power and terror spoke
In waves that on their iron coast-line broke?

Be it as it may: within the Land of Penn
The sectary yielded to the citizen,
And peaceful dwelt the many-creeded men.

Peace brooded over all. No trumpet stung

The air to madness, and no steeple flung
Alarums down from bells at midnight rung.

The land slept well. The Indian from his face
Washed all his war-paint off, and in the place
Of battle-marches sped the peaceful chase,

Or wrought for wages at the white man's side,
Giving to kindness what his native pride
And lazy freedom to all else denied.

And well the curious scholar loved the old
Traditions that his swarthy neighbors told
By wigwam-fires when nights were growing cold,

Discerned the fact round which their fancy drew
Its dreams, and held their childish faith more true
To God and man than half the creeds he knew.

The desert blossomed round him; wheat-fields rolled
Beneath the warm wind waves of green and gold;
The planted ear returned its hundred-fold.

Great clusters ripened in a warmer sun
Than that which by the Rhine stream shines upon
The purpling hillsides with low vines o'errun.

About each rustic porch the humming-bird
Tried with light bill, that scarce a petal stirred,
The Old World flowers to virgin soil transferred;

And the first-fruits of pear and apple, bending
The young boughs down, their gold and russet blending,
Made glad his heart, familiar odors lending

To the fresh fragrance of the birch and pine,
Life-everlasting, bay, and eglantine,
And all the subtle scents the woods combine.

Fair First-Day mornings, steeped in summer calm,
Warm, tender, restful, sweet with woodland balm,
Came to him, like some mother-hallowed psalm

To the tired grinder at the noisy wheel
Of labor, winding off from memory's reel
A golden thread of music. With no peal

Of bells to call them to the house of praise,
The scattered settlers through green forest-ways
Walked meeting-ward. In reverent amaze

The Indian trapper saw them, from the dim

Shade of the alders on the rivulet's rim,
Seek the Great Spirit's house to talk with Him.

There, through the gathered stillness multiplied
And made intense by sympathy, outside
The sparrows sang, and the gold-robin cried,

A-swing upon his elm. A faint perfume
Breathed through the open windows of the room
From locust-trees, heavy with clustered bloom.

Thither, perchance, sore-tried confessors came,
Whose fervor jail nor pillory could tame,
Proud of the cropped ears meant to be their shame,

Men who had eaten slavery's bitter bread
In Indian isles; pale women who had bled
Under the hangman's lash, and bravely said

God's message through their prison's iron bars;
And gray old soldier-converts, seamed with scars
From every stricken field of England's wars.

Lowly before the Unseen Presence knelt
Each waiting heart, till haply some one felt
On his moved lips the seal of silence melt.

Or, without spoken words, low breathings stole
Of a diviner life from soul to soul,
Baptizing in one tender thought the whole.

When shaken hands announced the meeting o'er,
The friendly group still lingered at the door,
Greeting, inquiring, sharing all the store

Of weekly tidings. Meanwhile youth and maid
Down the green vistas of the woodland strayed,
Whispered and smiled and oft their feet delayed.

Did the boy's whistle answer back the thrushes?
Did light girl laughter ripple through the bushes,
As brooks make merry over roots and rushes?

Unvexed the sweet air seemed. Without a wound
The ear of silence heard, and every sound
Its place in nature's fine accordance found.

And solemn meeting, summer sky and wood,
Old kindly faces, youth and maidenhood
Seemed, like God's new creation, very good!

And, greeting all with quiet smile and word,

Pastorius went his way. The unscared bird
Sang at his side; scarcely the squirrel stirred

At his hushed footstep on the mossy sod;
And, wheresoe'er the good man looked or trod,
He felt the peace of nature and of God.

His social life wore no ascetic form,
He loved all beauty, without fear of harm,
And in his veins his Teuton blood ran warm.

Strict to himself, of other men no spy,
He made his own no circuit-judge to try
The freer conscience of his neighbors by.

With love rebuking, by his life alone,
Gracious and sweet, the better way was shown,
The joy of one, who, seeking not his own,

And faithful to all scruples, finds at last
The thorns and shards of duty overpast,
And daily life, beyond his hope's forecast,

Pleasant and beautiful with sight and sound,
And flowers upspringing in its narrow round,
And all his days with quiet gladness crowned.

He sang not; but, if sometimes tempted strong,
He hummed what seemed like Altorf's Burschen-song;
His good wife smiled, and did not count it wrong.

For well he loved his boyhood's brother band;
His Memory, while he trod the New World's strand,
A double-ganger walked the Fatherland

If, when on frosty Christmas eves the light
Shone on his quiet hearth, he missed the sight
Of Yule-log, Tree, and Christ-child all in white;

And closed his eyes, and listened to the sweet
Old wait-songs sounding down his native street,
And watched again the dancers' mingling feet;

Yet not the less, when once the vision passed,
He held the plain and sober maxims fast
Of the dear Friends with whom his lot was cast.

Still all attuned to nature's melodies,
He loved the bird's song in his dooryard trees,
And the low hum of home-returning bees;

The blossomed flax, the tulip-trees in bloom

Down the long street, the beauty and perfume
Of apple-boughs, the mingling light and gloom

Of Sommerhausen's woodlands, woven through
With sun-threads; and the music the wind drew,
Mournful and sweet, from leaves it overblew.

And evermore, beneath this outward sense,
And through the common sequence of events,
He felt the guiding hand of Providence

Reach out of space. A Voice spake in his ear,
And to all other voices far and near
Died at that whisper, full of meanings clear.

The Light of Life shone round him; one by one
The wandering lights, that all-misleading run,
Went out like candles paling in the sun.

That Light he followed, step by step, where'er
It led, as in the vision of the seer
The wheels moved as the spirit in the clear

And terrible crystal moved, with all their eyes
Watching the living splendor sink or rise,
Its will their will, knowing no otherwise.

Within himself he found the law of right,
He walked by faith and not the letter's sight,
And read his Bible by the Inward Light.

And if sometimes the slaves of form and rule,
Frozen in their creeds like fish in winter's pool,
Tried the large tolerance of his liberal school,

His door was free to men of every name,
He welcomed all the seeking souls who came,
And no man's faith he made a cause of blame.

But best he loved in leisure hours to see
His own dear Friends sit by him knee to knee,
In social converse, genial, frank, and free.

There sometimes silence (it were hard to tell
Who owned it first) upon the circle fell,
Hushed Anna's busy wheel, and laid its spell

On the black boy who grimaced by the hearth,
To solemnize his shining face of mirth;
Only the old clock ticked amidst the dearth

Of sound; nor eye was raised nor hand was stirred

In that soul-sabbath, till at last some word
Of tender counsel or low prayer was heard.

Then guests, who lingered but farewell to say
And take love's message, went their homeward way;
So passed in peace the guileless Quaker's day.

His was the Christian's unsung Age of Gold,
A truer idyl than the bards have told
Of Arno's banks or Arcady of old.

Where still the Friends their place of burial keep,
And century-rooted mosses o'er it creep,
The Nurnberg scholar and his helpmeet sleep.

And Anna's aloe? If it flowered at last
In Bartram's garden, did John Woolman cast
A glance upon it as he meekly passed?

And did a secret sympathy possess
That tender soul, and for the slave's redress
Lend hope, strength, patience? It were vain to guess.

Nay, were the plant itself but mythical,
Set in the fresco of tradition's wall
Like Jotham's bramble, mattereth not at all.

Enough to know that, through the winter's frost
And summer's heat, no seed of truth is lost,
And every duty pays at last its cost.

For, ere Pastorius left the sun and air,
God sent the answer to his life-long prayer;
The child was born beside the Delaware,

Who, in the power a holy purpose lends,
Guided his people unto nobler ends,
And left them worthier of the name of Friends.

And to! the fulness of the time has come,
And over all the exile's Western home,
From sea to sea the flowers of freedom bloom!

And joy-bells ring, and silver trumpets blow;
But not for thee, Pastorius! Even so
The world forgets, but the wise angels know.

The Preacher
Its windows flashing to the sky,
Beneath a thousand roofs of brown,
Far down the vale, my friend and I

Beheld the old and quiet town;
The ghostly sails that out at sea
Flapped their white wings of mystery;
The beaches glimmering in the sun,
And the low wooded capes that run
Into the sea-mist north and south;
The sand-bluffs at the river's mouth;
The swinging chain-bridge, and, afar,
The foam-line of the harbor-bar.

Over the woods and meadow-lands
A crimson-tinted shadow lay,
Of clouds through which the setting day
Flung a slant glory far away.
It glittered on the wet sea-sands,
It flamed upon the city's panes,
Smote the white sails of ships that wore
Outward or in, and glided o'er
The steeples with their veering vanes!

Awhile my friend with rapid search
O'erran the landscape. 'Yonder spire
Over gray roofs, a shaft of fire;
What is it, pray?'-'The Whitefield Church!
Walled about by its basement stones,
There rest the marvellous prophet's bones.'
Then as our homeward way we walked,
Of the great preacher's life we talked;
And through the mystery of our theme
The outward glory seemed to stream,
And Nature's self interpreted
The doubtful record of the dead;
And every level beam that smote
The sails upon the dark afloat
A symbol of the light became,
Which touched the shadows of our blame,
With tongues of Pentecostal flame.

Over the roofs of the pioneers
Gathers the moss of a hundred years;
On man and his works has passed the change
Which needs must be in a century's range.
The land lies open and warm in the sun,
Anvils clamor and mill-wheels run,-
Flocks on the hillsides, herds on the plain,
The wilderness gladdened with fruit and grain!
But the living faith of the settlers old
A dead profession their children hold;
To the lust of office and greed of trade
A stepping-stone is the altar made.

The church, to place and power the door,

Rebukes the sin of the world no more,
Nor sees its Lord in the homeless poor.
Everywhere is the grasping hand,
And eager adding of land to land;
And earth, which seemed to the fathers meant
But as a pilgrim's wayside tent,
A nightly shelter to fold away
When the Lord should call at the break of day,
Solid and steadfast seems to be,
And Time has forgotten Eternity!

But fresh and green from the rotting roots
Of primal forests the young growth shoots;
From the death of the old the new proceeds,
And the life of truth from the rot of creeds
On the ladder of God, which upward leads,
The steps of progress are human needs.
For His judgments still are a mighty deep,
And the eyes of His providence never sleep
When the night is darkest He gives the morn;
When the famine is sorest, the wine and corn!

In the church of the wilderness Edwards wrought,
Shaping his creed at the forge of thought;
And with Thor's own hammer welded and bent
The iron links of his argument,
Which strove to grasp in its mighty span
The purpose of God and the fate of man
Yet faithful still, in his daily round
To the weak, and the poor, and sin-sick found,
The schoolman's lore and the casuist's art
Drew warmth and life from his fervent heart.

Had he not seen in the solitudes
Of his deep and dark Northampton woods
A vision of love about him fall?
Not the blinding splendor which fell on Saul,
But the tenderer glory that rests on them
Who walk in the New Jerusalem,
Where never the sun nor moon are known,
But the Lord and His love are the light alone
And watching the sweet, still countenance
Of the wife of his bosom rapt in trance,
Had he not treasured each broken word
Of the mystical wonder seen and heard;
And loved the beautiful dreamer more
That thus to the desert of earth she bore
Clusters of Eshcol from Canaan's shore?

As the barley-winnower, holding with pain
Aloft in waiting his chaff and grain,
Joyfully welcomes the far-off breeze

Sounding the pine-tree's slender keys,
So he who had waited long to hear
The sound of the Spirit drawing near,
Like that which the son of Iddo heard
When the feet of angels the myrtles stirred,
Felt the answer of prayer, at last,
As over his church the afflatus passed,
Breaking its sleep as breezes break
To sun-bright ripples a stagnant lake.

At first a tremor of silent fear,
The creep of the flesh at danger near,
A vague foreboding and discontent,
Over the hearts of the people went.
All nature warned in sounds and signs
The wind in the tops of the forest pines
In the name of the Highest called to prayer,
As the muezzin calls from the minaret stair.
Through ceiled chambers of secret sin
Sudden and strong the light shone in;
A guilty sense of his neighbor's needs
Startled the man of title-deeds;
The trembling hand of the worldling shook
The dust of years from the Holy Book;
And the psalms of David, forgotten long,
Took the place of the scoffer's song.

The impulse spread like the outward course
Of waters moved by a central force;
The tide of spiritual life rolled down
From inland mountains to seaboard town.

Prepared and ready the altar stands
Waiting the prophet's outstretched hands
And prayer availing, to downward call
The fiery answer in view of all.
Hearts are like wax in the furnace; who
Shall mould, and shape, and cast them anew?
Lo! by the Merrimac Whitefield stands
In the temple that never was made by hands,
Curtains of azure, and crystal wall,
And dome of the sunshine over all-
A homeless pilgrim, with dubious name
Blown about on the winds of fame;
Now as an angel of blessing classed,
And now as a mad enthusiast.
Called in his youth to sound and gauge
The moral lapse of his race and age,
And, sharp as truth, the contrast draw
Of human frailty and perfect law;
Possessed by the one dread thought that lent
Its goad to his fiery temperament,

Up and down the world he went,
A John the Baptist crying, Repent!

No perfect whole can our nature make;
Here or there the circle will break;
The orb of life as it takes the light
On one side leaves the other in night.
Never was saint so good and great
As to give no chance at St. Peter's gate
For the plea of the Devil's advocate.
So, incomplete by his being's law,
The marvellous preacher had his flaw;
With step unequal, and lame with faults,
His shade on the path of History halts.

Wisely and well said the Eastern bard
Fear is easy, but love is hard,
Easy to glow with the Santon's rage,
And walk on the Meccan pilgrimage;
But he is greatest and best who can
Worship Allah by loving man.
Thus he,-to whom, in the painful stress
Of zeal on fire from its own excess,
Heaven seemed so vast and earth so small
That man was nothing, since God was all,
Forgot, as the best at times have done,
That the love of the Lord and of man are one.
Little to him whose feet unshod
The thorny path of the desert trod,
Careless of pain, so it led to God,
Seemed the hunger-pang and the poor man's wrong,
The weak ones trodden beneath the strong.
Should the worm be chooser? the clay withstand
The shaping will of the potter's hand?

In the Indian fable Arjoon hears
The scorn of a god rebuke his fears
'Spare thy pity!' Krishna saith;
'Not in thy sword is the power of death!
All is illusion,-loss but seems;
Pleasure and pain are only dreams;
Who deems he slayeth doth not kill;
Who counts as slain is living still.
Strike, nor fear thy blow is crime;
Nothing dies but the cheats of time;
Slain or slayer, small the odds
To each, immortal as Indra's gods!'

So by Savannah's banks of shade,
The stones of his mission the preacher laid
On the heart of the negro crushed and rent,
And made of his blood the wall's cement;

Bade the slave-ship speed from coast to coast,
Fanned by the wings of the Holy Ghost;
And begged, for the love of Christ, the gold
Coined from the hearts in its groaning hold.
What could it matter, more or less
Of stripes, and hunger, and weariness?
Living or dying, bond or free,
What was time to eternity?

Alas for the preacher's cherished schemes!
Mission and church are now but dreams;
Nor prayer nor fasting availed the plan
To honor God through the wrong of man.
Of all his labors no trace remains
Save the bondman lifting his hands in chains.
The woof he wove in the righteous warp
Of freedom-loving Oglethorpe,
Clothes with curses the goodly land,
Changes its greenness and bloom to sand;
And a century's lapse reveals once more
The slave-ship stealing to Georgia's shore.
Father of Light! how blind is he
Who sprinkles the altar he rears to Thee
With the blood and tears of humanity!

He erred: shall we count His gifts as naught?
Was the work of God in him unwrought?
The servant may through his deafness err,
And blind may be God's messenger;
But the Errand is sure they go upon,
The word is spoken, the deed is done.
Was the Hebrew temple less fair and good
That Solomon bowed to gods of wood?
For his tempted heart and wandering feet,
Were the songs of David less pure and sweet?
So in light and shadow the preacher went,
God's erring and human instrument;
And the hearts of the people where he passed
Swayed as the reeds sway in the blast,
Under the spell of a voice which took
In its compass the flow of Siloa's brook,
And the mystical chime of the bells of gold
On the ephod's hem of the priest of old,
Now the roll of thunder, and now the awe
Of the trumpet heard in the Mount of Law.

A solemn fear on the listening crowd
Fell like the shadow of a cloud.
The sailor reeling from out the ships
Whose masts stood thick in the river-slips
Felt the jest and the curse die on his lips.
Listened the fisherman rude and hard,

The calker rough from the builder's yard;
The man of the market left his load,
The teamster leaned on his bending goad,
The maiden, and youth beside her, felt
Their hearts in a closer union melt,
And saw the flowers of their love in bloom
Down the endless vistas of life to come.
Old age sat feebly brushing away
From his ears the scanty locks of gray;
And careless boyhood, living the free
Unconscious life of bird and tree,
Suddenly wakened to a sense
Of sin and its guilty consequence.
It was as if an angel's voice
Called the listeners up for their final choice;
As if a strong hand rent apart
The veils of sense from soul and heart,
Showing in light ineffable
The joys of heaven and woes of hell
All about in the misty air
The hills seemed kneeling in silent prayer;
The rustle of leaves, the moaning sedge,
The water's lap on its gravelled edge,
The wailing pines, and, far and faint,
The wood-dove's note of sad complaint,
To the solemn voice of the preacher lent
An undertone as of low lament;
And the note of the sea from its sand coast,
On the easterly wind, now heard, now lost,
Seemed the murmurous sound of the judgment host.

Yet wise men doubted, and good men wept,
As that storm of passion above them swept,
And, comet-like, adding flame to flame,
The priests of the new Evangel came,
Davenport, flashing upon the crowd,
Charged like summer's electric cloud,
Now holding the listener still as death
With terrible warnings under breath,
Now shouting for joy, as if he viewed
The vision of Heaven's beatitude!
And Celtic Tennant, his long coat bound
Like a monk's with leathern girdle round,
Wild with the toss of unshorn hair,
And wringing of hands, and, eyes aglare,
Groaning under the world's despair!
Grave pastors, grieving their flocks to lose,
Prophesied to the empty pews
That gourds would wither, and mushrooms die,
And noisiest fountains run soonest dry,
Like the spring that gushed in Newbury Street,
Under the tramp of the earthquake's feet,

A silver shaft in the air and light,
For a single day, then lost in night,
Leaving only, its place to tell,
Sandy fissure and sulphurous smell.
With zeal wing-clipped and white-heat cool,
Moved by the spirit in grooves of rule,
No longer harried, and cropped, and fleeced,
Flogged by sheriff and cursed by priest,
But by wiser counsels left at ease
To settle quietly on his lees,
And, self-concentred, to count as done
The work which his fathers well begun,
In silent protest of letting alone,
The Quaker kept the way of his own,
A non-conductor among the wires,
With coat of asbestos proof to fires.
And quite unable to mend his pace
To catch the falling manna of grace,
He hugged the closer his little store
Of faith, and silently prayed for more.
And vague of creed and barren of rite,
But holding, as in his Master's sight,
Act and thought to the inner light,
The round of his simple duties walked,
And strove to live what the others talked.

And who shall marvel if evil went
Step by step with the good intent,
And with love and meekness, side by side,
Lust of the flesh and spiritual pride?-
That passionate longings and fancies vain
Set the heart on fire and crazed the brain?
That over the holy oracles
Folly sported with cap and bells?
That goodly women and learned men
Marvelling told with tongue and pen
How unweaned children chirped like birds
Texts of Scripture and solemn words,
Like the infant seers of the rocky glens
In the Puy de Dome of wild Cevennes
Or baby Lamas who pray and preach
From Tartir cradles in Buddha's speech?

In the war which Truth or Freedom wages
With impious fraud and the wrong of ages,
Hate and malice and self-love mar
The notes of triumph with painful jar,
And the helping angels turn aside
Their sorrowing faces the shame to bide.
Never on custom's oiled grooves
The world to a higher level moves,
But grates and grinds with friction hard

On granite boulder and flinty shard.
The heart must bleed before it feels,
The pool be troubled before it heals;
Ever by losses the right must gain,
Every good have its birth of pain;
The active Virtues blush to find
The Vices wearing their badge behind,
And Graces and Charities feel the fire
Wherein the sins of the age expire;
The fiend still rends as of old he rent
The tortured body from which be went.

But Time tests all. In the over-drift
And flow of the Nile, with its annual gift,
Who cares for the Hadji's relics sunk?
Who thinks of the drowned-out Coptic monk?
The tide that loosens the temple's stones,
And scatters the sacred ibis-bones,
Drives away from the valley-land
That Arab robber, the wandering sand,
Moistens the fields that know no rain,
Fringes the desert with belts of grain,
And bread to the sower brings again.
So the flood of emotion deep and strong
Troubled the land as it swept along,
But left a result of holier lives,
Tenderer-mothers and worthier wives.
The husband and father whose children fled
And sad wife wept when his drunken tread
Frightened peace from his roof-tree's shade,
And a rock of offence his hearthstone made,
In a strength that was not his own began
To rise from the brute's to the plane of man.
Old friends embraced, long held apart
By evil counsel and pride of heart;
And penitence saw through misty tears,
In the bow of hope on its cloud of fears,
The promise of Heaven's eternal years,
The peace of God for the world's annoy,
Beauty for ashes, and oil of joy
Under the church of Federal Street,
Under the tread of its Sabbath feet,
Walled about by its basement stones,
Lie the marvellous preacher's bones.
No saintly honors to them are shown,
No sign nor miracle have they known;
But be who passes the ancient church
Stops in the shade of its belfry-porch,
And ponders the wonderful life of him
Who lies at rest in that charnel dim.
Long shall the traveller strain his eye
From the railroad car, as it plunges by,

And the vanishing town behind him search
For the slender spire of the Whitefield Church;
And feel for one moment the ghosts of trade,
And fashion, and folly, and pleasure laid,
By the thought of that life of pure intent,
That voice of warning yet eloquent,
Of one on the errands of angels sent.
And if where he labored the flood of sin
Like a tide from the harbor-bar sets in,
And over a life of tune and sense
The church-spires lift their vain defence,
As if to scatter the bolts of God
With the points of Calvin's thunder-rod,
Still, as the gem of its civic crown,
Precious beyond the world's renown,
His memory hallows the ancient town!

The Proclamation
Saint Patrick, slave to Milcho of the herds
Of Ballymena, wakened with these words:
'Arise, and flee
Out from the land of bondage, and be free!'
Glad as a soul in pain, who hears from heaven
The angels singing of his sins forgiven,
And, wondering, sees
His prison opening to their golden keys,
He rose a man who laid him down a slave,
Shook from his locks the ashes of the grave,
And outward trod
Into the glorious liberty of God.
He east the symbols of his shame away;
And, passing where the sleeping Milcho lay,
Though back and limb
Smarted with wrong, he prayed, 'God pardon him!'
So went he forth; but in God's time he came
To light on Uilline's hills a holy flame;
And, dying, gave
The land a saint that lost him as a slave.
O dark, sad millions, patiently and dumb
Waiting for God, your hour at last has come,
And freedom's song
Breaks the long silence of your night of wrong!
Arise and flee! shake off the vile restraint
Of ages; but, like Ballymena's saint,
The oppressor spare,
Heap only on his head the coals of prayer.
Go forth, like him! like him return again,
To bless the land whereon in bitter pain
Ye toiled at first,
And heal with freedom what your slavery cursed.

The Prophecy Of Samuel Sewall

Up and down the village streets
Strange are the forms my fancy meets,
For the thoughts and things of to-day are hid,
And through the veil of a closed lid
The ancient worthies I see again
I hear the tap of the elder's cane,
And his awful periwig I see,
And the silver buckles of shoe and knee.
Stately and slow, with thoughtful air,
His black cap hiding his whitened hair,
Walks the Judge of the great Assize,
Samuel Sewall the good and wise.
His face with lines of firmness wrought,
He wears the look of a man unbought,
Who swears to his hurt and changes not;
Yet, touched and softened nevertheless
With the grace of Christian gentleness,
The face that a child would climb to kiss!
True and tender and brave and just,
That man might honor and woman trust.

Touching and sad, a tale is told,
Like a penitent hymn of the Psalmist old,
Of the fast which the good man lifelong kept to
With a haunting sorrow that never slept,
As the circling year brought round the time
Of an error that left the sting of crime,
When he sat on the bench of the witchcraft courts,
With the laws of Moses and Hale's Reports,
And spake, in the name of both, the word
That gave the witch's neck to the cord,
And piled the oaken planks that pressed
The feeble life from the warlock's breast!
All the day long, from dawn to dawn,
His door was bolted, his curtain drawn;
No foot on his silent threshold trod,
No eye looked on him save that of God,
As he baffled the ghosts of the dead with charms
Of penitent tears, and prayers, and psalms,
And, with precious proofs from the sacred word
Of the boundless pity and love of the Lord,
His faith confirmed and his trust renewed
That the sin of his ignorance, sorely rued,
Might be washed away in the mingled flood
Of his human sorrow and Christ's dear blood!

Green forever the memory be
Of the Judge of the old Theocracy,
Whom even his errors glorified,
Like a far-seen, sunlit mountain-side

By the cloudy shadows which o'er it glide I
Honor and praise to the Puritan
Who the halting step of his age outran,
And, seeing the infinite worth of man
In the priceless gift the Father gave,
In the infinite love that stooped to save,
Dared not brand his brother a slave
'Who doth such wrong,' he was wont to say,
In his own quaint, picture-loving way,
'Flings up to Heaven a hand-grenade
Which God shall cast down upon his head!'

Widely as heaven and hell, contrast
That brave old jurist of the past
And the cunning trickster and knave of courts
Who the holy features of Truth distorts,
Ruling as right the will of the strong,
Poverty, crime, and weakness wrong;
Wide-eared to power, to the wronged and weak
Deaf as Egypt's gods of leek;
Scoffing aside at party's nod
Order of nature and law of God;
For whose dabbled ermine respect were waste,
Reverence folly, and awe misplaced;
Justice of whom 't were vain to seek
As from Koordish robber or Syrian Sheik!
Oh, leave the wretch to his bribes and sins!
Let him rot in the web of lies he spins!
To the saintly soul of the early day,
To the Christian judge, let us turn and say
'Praise and thanks for an honest man!
Glory to God for the Puritan!'

I see, far southward, this quiet day,
The hills of Newbury rolling away,
With the many tints of the season gay,
Dreamily blending in autumn mist
Crimson, and gold, and amethyst.
Long and low, with dwarf trees crowned,
Plum Island lies, like a whale aground,
A stone's toss over the narrow sound.
Inland, as far as the eye can go,
The hills curve round like a bended bow;
A silver arrow from out them sprung,
I see the shine of the Quasycung;
And, round and round, over valley and hill,
Old roads winding, as old roads will,
Here to a ferry, and there to a mill;
And glimpses of chimneys and gabled eaves,
Through green elm arches and maple leaves,
Old homesteads sacred to all that can
Gladden or sadden the heart of man,

Over whose thresholds of oak and stone
Life and Death have come and gone
There pictured tiles in the fireplace show,
Great beams sag from the ceiling low,
The dresser glitters with polished wares,
The long clock ticks on the foot-worn stairs,
And the low, broad chimney shows the crack
By the earthquake made a century back.
Up from their midst springs the village spire
With the crest of its cock in the sun afire;
Beyond are orchards and planting lands,
And great salt marshes and glimmering sands,
And, where north and south the coast-lines run,
The blink of the sea in breeze and sun!

I see it all like a chart unrolled,
But my thoughts are full of the past and old,
I hear the tales of my boyhood told;
And the shadows and shapes of early days
Flit dimly by in the veiling haze,
With measured movement and rhythmic chime
Weaving like shuttles my web of rhyme.
I think of the old man wise and good
Who once on yon misty hillsides stood,
(A poet who never measured rhyme,
A seer unknown to his dull-eared time,)
And, propped on his staff of age, looked down,
With his boyhood's love, on his native town,
Where, written, as if on its hills and plains,
His burden of prophecy yet remains,
For the voices of wood, and wave, and wind
To read in the ear of the musing mind:

'As long as Plum Island, to guard the coast
As God appointed, shall keep its post;
As long as a salmon shall haunt the deep
Of Merrimac River, or sturgeon leap;
As long as pickerel swift and slim,
Or red-backed perch, in Crane Pond swim;
As long as the annual sea-fowl know
Their time to come and their time to go;
As long as cattle shall roam at will
The green, grass meadows by Turkey Hill;
As long as sheep shall look from the side
Of Oldtown Hill on marshes wide,
And Parker River, and salt-sea tide;
As long as a wandering pigeon shall search
The fields below from his white-oak perch,
When the barley-harvest is ripe and shorn,
And the dry husks fall from the standing corn;
As long as Nature shall not grow old,
Nor drop her work from her doting hold,

And her care for the Indian corn forget,
And the yellow rows in pairs to set;
So long shall Christians here be born,
Grow up and ripen as God's sweet corn!
By the beak of bird, by the breath of frost,
Shall never a holy ear be lost,
But, husked by Death in the Planter's sight,
Be sown again in the fields of light!'

The Island still is purple with plums,
Up the river the salmon comes,
The sturgeon leaps, and the wild-fowl feeds
On hillside berries and marish seeds,
All the beautiful signs remain,
From spring-time sowing to autumn rain
The good man's vision returns again!
And let us hope, as well we can,
That the Silent Angel who garners man
May find some grain as of old lie found
In the human cornfield ripe and sound,
And the Lord of the Harvest deign to own
The precious seed by the fathers sown!

The Quaker Alumni
From the well-springs of Hudson, the sea-cliffs of Maine,
Grave men, sober matrons, you gather again;
And, with hearts warmer grown as your heads grow more cool,
Play over the old game of going to school.

All your strifes and vexations, your whims and complaints,
(You were not saints yourselves, if the children of saints!)
All your petty self-seekings and rivalries done,
Round the dear Alma Mater your hearts beat as one!

How widely soe'er you have strayed from the fold,
Though your 'thee' has grown 'you,' and your drab blue and gold,
To the old friendly speech and the garb's sober form,
Like the heart of Argyle to the tartan, you warm.

But, the first greetings over, you glance round the hall;
Your hearts call the roll, but they answer not all
Through the turf green above them the dead cannot hear;
Name by name, in the silence, falls sad as a tear!

In love, let us trust, they were summoned so soon
rom the morning of life, while we toil through its noon;
They were frail like ourselves, they had needs like our own,
And they rest as we rest in God's mercy alone.

Unchanged by our changes of spirit and frame,
Past, now, and henceforward the Lord is the same;

Though we sink in the darkness, His arms break our fall,
And in death as in life, He is Father of all!

We are older: our footsteps, so light in the play
Of the far-away school-time, move slower to-day;
Here a beard touched with frost, there a bald, shining crown,
And beneath the cap's border gray mingles with brown.

But faith should be cheerful, and trust should be glad,
And our follies and sins, not our years, make us sad.
Should the heart closer shut as the bonnet grows prim,
And the face grow in length as the hat grows in brim?

Life is brief, duty grave; but, with rain-folded wings,
Of yesterday's sunshine the grateful heart sings;
And we, of all others, have reason to pay
The tribute of thanks, and rejoice on our way;

For the counsels that turned from the follies of youth;
For the beauty of patience, the whiteness of truth;
For the wounds of rebuke, when love tempered its edge;
For the household's restraint, and the discipline's hedge;

For the lessons of kindness vouchsafed to the least
Of the creatures of God, whether human or beast,
Bringing hope to the poor, lending strength to the frail,
In the lanes of the city, the slave-hut, and jail;

For a womanhood higher and holier, by all
Her knowledge of good, than was Eve ere her fall,
Whose task-work of duty moves lightly as play,
Serene as the moonlight and warm as the day;

And, yet more, for the faith which embraces the whole,
Of the creeds of the ages the life and the soul,
Wherein letter and spirit the same channel run,
And man has not severed what God has made one!

For a sense of the Goodness revealed everywhere,
As sunshine impartial, and free as the air;
For a trust in humanity, Heathen or Jew,
And a hope for all darkness the Light shineth through.

Who scoffs at our birthright? the words of the seers,
And the songs of the bards in the twilight of years,
All the foregleams of wisdom in santon and sage,
In prophet and priest, are our true heritage.

The Word which the reason of Plato discerned;
The truth, as whose symbol the Mithra-fire burned;
The soul of the world which the Stoic but guessed,
In the Light Universal the Quaker confessed!

No honors of war to our worthies belong;
Their plain stem of life never flowered into song;
But the fountains they opened still gush by the way,
And the world for their healing is better to-day.

He who lies where the minster's groined arches curve down
To the tomb-crowded transept of England's renown,
The glorious essayist, by genius enthroned,
Whose pen as a sceptre the Muses all owned,

Who through the world's pantheon walked in his pride,
Setting new statues up, thrusting old ones aside,
And in fiction the pencils of history dipped,
To gild o'er or blacken each saint in his crypt,

How vainly he labored to sully with blame
The white bust of Penn, in the niche of his fame!
Self-will is self-wounding, perversity blind
On himself fell the stain for the Quaker designed!

For the sake of his true-hearted father before him;
For the sake of the dear Quaker mother that bore him;
For the sake of his gifts, and the works that outlive him,
And his brave words for freedom, we freely forgive him!

There are those who take note that our numbers are small,
New Gibbons who write our decline and our fall;
But the Lord of the seed-field takes care of His own,
And the world shall yet reap what our sowers have sown.

The last of the sect to his fathers may go,
Leaving only his coat for some Barnum to show;
But the truth will outlive him, and broaden with years,
Till the false dies away, and the wrong disappears.

Nothing fails of its end. Out of sight sinks the stone,
In the deep sea of time, but the circles sweep on,
Till the low-rippled murmurs along the shores run,
And the dark and dead waters leap glad in the sun.

Meanwhile shall we learn, in our ease, to forget
To the martyrs of Truth and of Freedom our debt?
Hide their words out of sight, like the garb that they wore,
And for Barclay's Apology offer one more?

Shall we fawn round the priestcraft that glutted the shears,
And festooned the stocks with our grandfathers' ears?
Talk of Woolman's unsoundness? count Penn heterodox?
And take Cotton Mather in place of George Fox?

Make our preachers war-chaplains? quote Scripture to take

The hunted slave back, for Onesimus' sake?
Go to burning church-candles, and chanting in choir,
And on the old meeting-house stick up a spire?

No! the old paths we'll keep until better are shown,
Credit good where we find it, abroad or our own;
And while 'Lo here' and 'Lo there' the multitude call,
Be true to ourselves, and do justice to all.

The good round about us we need not refuse,
Nor talk of our Zion as if we were Jews;
But why shirk the badge which our fathers have worn,
Or beg the world's pardon for having been born?

We need not pray over the Pharisee's prayer,
Nor claim that our wisdom is Benjamin's share;
Truth to us and to others is equal and one
Shall we bottle the free air, or hoard up the sun?

Well know we our birthright may serve but to show
How the meanest of weeds in the richest soil grow;
But we need not disparage the good which we hold;
Though the vessels be earthen, the treasure is gold!

Enough and too much of the sect and the name.
What matters our label, so truth be our aim?
The creed may be wrong, but the life may be true,
And hearts beat the same under drab coats or blue.

So the man be a man, let him worship, at will,
In Jerusalem's courts, or on Gerizim's hill.
When she makes up her jewels, what cares yon good town
For the Baptist of Wayland, the Quaker of Brown?

And this green, favored island, so fresh and seablown,
When she counts up the worthies her annals have known,
Never waits for the pitiful gaugers of sect
To measure her love, and mete out her respect.

Three shades at this moment seem walking her strand,
Each with head halo-crowned, and with palms in his hand,
Wise Berkeley, grave Hopkins, and, smiling serene
On prelate and puritan, Channing is seen.

One holy name bearing, no longer they need
Credentials of party, and pass-words of creed
The new song they sing hath a threefold accord,
And they own one baptism, one faith, and one Lord!

But the golden sands run out: occasions like these
Glide swift into shadow, like sails on the seas
While we sport with the mosses and pebbles ashore,

They lessen and fade, and we see them no more.

Forgive me, dear friends, if my vagrant thoughts seem
Like a school-boy's who idles and plays with his theme.
Forgive the light measure whose changes display
The sunshine and rain of our brief April day.

There are moments in life when the lip and the eye
Try the question of whether to smile or to cry;
And scenes and reunions that prompt like our own
The tender in feeling, the playful in tone.

I, who never sat down with the boys and the girls
At the feet of your Slocums, and Cartlands, and Earles,
By courtesy only permitted to lay
On your festival's altar my poor gift, to-day,

I would joy in your joy: let me have a friend's part
In the warmth of your welcome of hand and of heart,
On your play-ground of boyhood unbend the brow's care,
And shift the old burdens our shoulders must bear.

Long live the good School! giving out year by year
Recruits to true manhood and womanhood dear
Brave boys, modest maidens, in beauty sent forth,
The living epistles and proof of its worth!

In and out let the young life as steadily flow
As in broad Narragansett the tides come and go;
And its sons and its daughters in prairie and town
Remember its honor, and guard its renown.

Not vainly the gift of its founder was made;
Not prayerless the stones of its corner were laid
The blessing of Him whom in secret they sought
Has owned the good work which the fathers have wrought.

To Him be the glory forever! We bear
To the Lord of the Harvest our wheat with the tare.
What we lack in our work may He find in our will,
And winnow in mercy our good from the ill!

The Reformer
All grim and soiled and brown with tan,
I saw a Strong One, in his wrath,
Smiting the godless shrines of man
Along his path.
The Church, beneath her trembling dome,
Essayed in vain her ghostly charm:
Wealth shook within his gilded home
With strange alarm.

Fraud from his secret chambers fled
Before the sunlight bursting in:
Sloth drew her pillow o'er her head
To drown the din.
'Spare,' Art implored, 'yon holy pile;
That grand, old, time-worn turret spare;'
Meek Reverence, kneeling in the aisle,
Cried out, 'Forbear!'
Gray-bearded Use, who, deaf and blind,
Groped for his old accustomed stone,
Leaned on his staff, and wept to find
His seat o'erthrown.
Young Romance raised his dreamy eyes,
O'erhung with paly locks of gold,
'Why smite,' he asked in sad surprise,
'The fair, the old?'
Yet louder rang the Strong One's stroke,
Yet nearer flashed his axe's gleam;
Shuddering and sick of heart I woke,
As from a dream.
I looked: aside the dust-cloud rolled,
The Waster seemed the Builder too;
Upspringing from the ruined Old
I saw the New.
'T was but the ruin of the bad,
The wasting of the wrong and ill;
Whate'er of good the old time had
Was living still.
Calm grew the brows of him I feared;
The frown which awed me passed away,
And left behind a smile which cheered
Like breaking day.
The grain grew green on battle-plains,
O'er swarded war-mounds grazed the cow;
The slave stood forging from his chains
The spade and plough.
Where frowned the fort, pavilions gay
And cottage windows, flower-entwined,
Looked out upon the peaceful bay
And hills behind.
Through vine-wreathed cups with wine once red,
The lights on brimming crystal fell,
Drawn, sparkling, from the rivulet head
And mossy well.
Through prison walls, like Heaven-sent hope,
Fresh breezes blew, and sunbeams strayed,
And with the idle gallows-rope
The young child played.
Where the doomed victim in his cell
Had counted o'er the weary hours,
Glad school-girls, answering to the bell,
Came crowed with flowers.

Grown wiser for the lesson given,
I fear no longer, for I know
That, where the share is deepest driven,
The best fruits grow.
The outworn rite, the old abuse,
The pious fraud transparent grown,
The good held captive in the use
Of wrong alone,
These wait their doom, from that great law
Which makes the past time serve to-day;
And fresher life the world shall draw
From their decay.
Oh, backward-looking son of time!
The new is old, the old is new,
The cycle of a change sublime
Still sweeping through.
So wisely taught the Indian seer;
Destroying Seva, forming Brahm,
Who wake by turns Earth's love and fear,
Are one, the same.
Idly as thou, in that old day
Thou mournest, did thy sire repine;
So, in his time, thy child grown gray
Shall sigh for thine.
But life shall on and upward go;
Th' eternal step of Progress beats
To that great anthem, calm and slow,
Which God repeats.
Take heart! the Waster builds again,
A charmëd life old Goodness hath;
The tares may perish, but the grain
Is not for death.
God works in all things; all obey
His first propulsion from the night:
Wake thou and watch! the world is gray
With morning light!

The Relic

Token of friendship true and tried,
From one whose fiery heart of youth
With mine has beaten, side by side,
For Liberty and Truth;
With honest pride the gift I take,
And prize it for the giver's sake.
But not alone because it tells
Of generous hand and heart sincere;
Around that gift of friendship dwells
A memory doubly dear;
Earth's noblest aim, man's holiest thought,
With that memorial frail inwrought!
Pure thoughts and sweet like flowers unfold,

And precious memories round it cling,
Even as the Prophet's rod of old
In beauty blossoming:
And buds of feeling, pure and good,
Spring from its cold unconscious wood.
Relic of Freedom's shrine! a brand
Plucked from its burning! let it be
Dear as a jewel from the hand
Of a lost friend to me!
Flower of a perished garland left,
Of life and beauty unbereft!
Oh, if the young enthusiast bears,
O'er weary waste and sea, the stone
Which crumbled from the Forum's stairs,
Or round the Parthenon;
Or olive-bough from some wild tree
Hung over old Thermopylæ:
If leaflets from some hero's tomb,
Or moss-wreath torn from ruins hoary;
Or faded flowers whose sisters bloom
On fields renowned in story;
Or fragment from the Alhambra's crest,
Or the gray rock by Druids blessed;
Sad Erin's shamrock greenly growing
Where Freedom led her stalwart kern,
Or Scotia's 'rough bur thistle' blowing
On Bruce's Bannockburn;
Or Runnymede's wild English rose,
Or lichen plucked from Sempach's snows!
If it be true that things like these
To heart and eye bright visions bring,
Shall not far holier memories
To this memorial cling?
Which needs no mellowing mist of time
To hide the crimson stains of crime!
Wreck of a temple, unprofaned;
Of courts where Peace with Freedom trod,
Lifting on high, with hands unstained,
Thanksgiving unto God;
Where Mercy's voice of love was pleading
For human hearts in bondage bleeding!
Where, midst the sound of rushing feet
And curses on the night-air flung,
That pleading voice rose calm and sweet
From woman's earnest tongue;
And Riot turned his scowling glance,
Awed, from her tranquil countenance!
That temple now in ruin lies!
The fire-stain on its shattered wall,
And open to the changing skies
Its black and roofless hall,
It stands before a nation's sight

A gravestone over buried Right!
But from that ruin, as of old,
The fire-scorched stones themselves are crying,
And from their ashes white and cold
Its timbers are replying!
A voice which slavery cannot kill
Speaks from the crumbling arches still!
And even this relic from thy shrine,
O holy Freedom! hath to me
A potent power, a voice and sign
To testify of thee;
And, grasping it, methinks I feel
A deeper faith, a stronger zeal.
And not unlike that mystic rod,
Of old stretched o'er the Egyptian wave,
Which opened, in the strength of God,
A pathway for the slave,
It yet may point the bondman's way,
And turn the spoiler from his prey.

The Sentence Of John L. Brown

Ho! thou who seekest late and long
A License from the Holy Book
For brutal lust and fiendish wrong,
Man of the Pulpit, look!
Lift up those cold and atheist eyes,
This ripe fruit of thy teaching see;
And tell us how to heaven will rise
The incense of this sacrifice
This blossom of the gallows tree!
Search out for slavery's hour of need
Some fitting text of sacred writ;
Give heaven the credit of deed
Which shames the nether pit.
Kneel, smooth blasphemer, unto Him
Whose truth is on thy lips a lie;
Ask that His bright winged cherubim
May bend around that scaffold grim
To guard and bless and sanctify.
O champion of the people's cause!
Suspend thy loud and vain rebuke
Of foreign wrong and Old World's laws,
Man of the Senate, look!
Was this the promise of the free,
The great hope of our early time,
That slavery's poison vine should be
Upborne by Freedom's prayer-nursed tree
O'erclustered with such fruits of crime?
Send out the summons East and West,
And South and North, let all be there
Where he who pitied the oppressed

Swings out in sun and air.
Let not a Democratic hand
The grisly hangman's task refuse;
There let each loyal patriot stand,
Awaiting slavery's command,
To twist the rope and draw the noose!
But vain is irony — unmeet
Its cold rebuke for deeds which start
In fiery and indignant beat
The pulses of the heart.
Leave studied wit and guarded phrase
For those who think but do not feel;
Let men speak out in words which raise
Where'er they fall, an answering blaze
Like flints which strike the fire from steel.
Still let a mousing priesthood ply
Their garbled text and gloss of sin,
And make the lettered scroll deny
Its living soul within:
Still let the place-fed, titled knave
Plead robbery's right with purchased lips,
And tell us that our fathers gave
For Freedom's pedestal, a slave,
The frieze and moulding, chains and whips!
But ye who own that Higher Law
Whose tablets in the heart are set,
Speak out in words of power and awe
That God is living yet!
Breathe forth once more those tones sublime
Which thrilled the burdened prophet's lyre,
And in a dark and evil time
Smote down on Israel's fast of crime
And gift of blood, a rain of fire!
Oh, not for us the graceful lay
To whose soft measures lightly move
The footsteps of the faun and fay,
O'er-locked by mirth and love!
But such a stern and startling strain
As Britain's hunted bards flung down
From Snowden to the conquered plain,
Where harshly clanked the Saxon chain,
On trampled field and smoking town.
By Liberty's dishonored name,
By man's lost hope and failing trust,
By words and deeds which bow with shame
Our foreheads to the dust,
By the exulting strangers' sneer,
Borne to us from the Old World's thrones,
And by their victims' grief who hear,
In sunless mines and dungeons drear,
How Freedom's land her faith disowns!
Speak out in acts. The time for words

Has passed, and deeds suffice alone;
In vain against the clang of swords
The wailing pipe is blown!
Act, act in God's name, while ye may!
Smite from the church her leprous limb!
Throw open to the light of day.
The bondman's cell, and break away
The chains the state has bound on him!
Ho! every true and living soul,
To Freedom's perilled altar bear
The Freeman's and the Christian's whole
Tongue, pen, and vote, and prayer!
One last, great battle for the right
One short, sharp struggle to be free!
To do is to succeed — our fight
Is waged in Heaven's approving sight;
The smile of God is Victory.

The Slave Ships

'All ready?' cried the captain;
'Ay, ay!' the seamen said;
'Heave up the worthless lubbers,
The dying and the dead.'
Up from the slave-ship's prison
Fierce, bearded heads were thrust
'Now let the sharks look to it,
Toss up the dead ones first!'
Corpse after corpse came.up,
Death had been busy there;
Where every blow is mercy,
Why should the spoiler spare?
Corpse after corpse they cast
Sullenly from the ship,
Yet bloody with the traces
Of fetter-link and whip.
Gloomily stood the captain,
With his arms upon his breast,
With his cold brow sternly knotted,
And his iron lip compressed.
'Are all the dead dogs over?'
Growled through that matted lip;
'The blind ones are no better,
Let's lighten the good ship.'
Hark! from the ship's dark bosom,
The very sounds of hell!
The ringing clank of iron,
The maniac's short, sharp yell!
The hoarse, low curse, throat-stified;
The starving infant's moan,
The horror of a breaking heart
Poured through a mother's groan.

Up from that loathsome prison
The stricken blind ones came:
Below, had all been darkness,
Above, was still the same.
Yet the holy breath of heaven
Was sweetly breathing there,
And the heated brow of fever
Cooled in the soft sea air.
'Overboard with them, shipmates!'
Cutlass and dirk were plied;
Fettered and blind, one after one,
Plunged down the vessel's side.
The sabre smote above,.
Beneath, the lean shark lay,
Waiting with wide and bloody jaw
His quick and human prey.
God of the earth! what cries
Rang upward unto thee?
Voices of agony and blood,
From ship-deck and from sea.
The last dull plunge was heard,
The last wave caught its stain,
And the unsated shark looked up
For human hearts in vain.

Red glowed the western waters,
The setting sun was there,
Scattering alike on wave and cloud
His fiery mesh of hair.
Amidst a group in blindness,
A solitary eye
Gazed, from the burdened slaver's deck,
Into that burning sky.
' A storm,' spoke out the gazer,
'Is gathering and at hand;
Curse on't, I'd give my other eye
For one firm rood of land.'
And then he laughed, but only
His echoed laugh replied,
For the blinded and the suffering
Alone were at his side.
Night settled on the waters,
And on a stormy heaven,
While fiercely on that lone ship's track
The thunder-gust was driven.
'A sail! — thank God, a sail!'
And as the helmsman spoke,
Up through the stormy murmur
A shout of gladness broke.
Down came the stranger vessel,
Unheeding on her way,
So near that on the slaver's deck

Fell off her driven spray.
' Ho! for the love of mercy,
We're perishing and blind!'
A wail of utter agony
Came back upon the wind:
' Help us! for we are stricken
With blindness every one;
Ten days we've floated fearfully,
Unnoting star or sun.
Our ship's the slaver Leon,
We're but a score on board;
Our slaves are all gone over,
Help, for the love of God!'
On livid brows of agony
The broad red lightning shone;
But the roar of wind and thunder
Stifled the answering groan;
Wailed from the broken waters
A last despairing cry,
As, kindling in the stormy light,
The stranger ship went by.

In the sunny Guadaloupe
A dark-hulled vessel lay,
With a crew who noted never
The nightfall or the day.
The blossom of the orange
Was white by every stream,
And tropic leaf, and flower, and bird
Were in the warm sunbeam.
And the sky was bright as ever,
And the moonlight slept as well,
On the palm-trees by the hillside,
And the streamlet of the dell:
And the glances of the Creole
Were still as archly deep,
And her smiles as full as ever
Of passion and of sleep.
But vain were bird and blossom,
The green earth and the sky,
And the smile of human faces,
To the slaver's darkened eye;
At the breaking of the morning,
At the star-lit evening time,
O'er a world of light and beauty
Fell the blackness of his crime.

The Slaves Of Martinique
Beams of noon, like burning lances, through the tree-tops flash and glisten,
As she stands before her lover, with raised face to look and listen.
Dark, but comely, like the maiden in the ancient Jewish song:

Scarcely has the toil of task-fields done her graceful beauty wrong.
He, the strong one and the manly, with the vassal's garb and hue,
Holding still his spirit's birthright, to his higher nature true;
Hiding deep the strengthening purpose of a freeman in his heart,
As the gregree holds his Fetich from the white man's gaze apart.
Ever foremost of his comrades, when the driver's morning horn
Calls away to stifling mill-house, to the fields of cane and corn:
Fall the keen and burning lashes never on his back or limb;
Scarce with look or word of censure, turns the driver unto him.
Yet, his brow is always thoughtful, and his eye is hard and stern;
Slavery's last and humblest lesson he has never deigned to learn.
And, at evening, when his comrades dance before their master's door,
Folding arms and knitting forehead, stands he silent evermore.
God be praised for every instinct which rebels against a lot
Where the brute survives the human, and man's upright form is not!
As the serpent-like bejuco winds his spiral fold on fold
Round the tall and stately ceiba, till it withers in his hold;
Slow decays the forest monarch, closer girds the fell embrace,
Till the tree is seen no longer, and the vine is in its place;
So a base and bestial nature round the vassal's manhood twines,
And the spirit wastes beneath it, like the ceiba choked with vines.
God is Love, saith the Evangel; and our world of woe and sin
Is made light and happy only when a Love is shining in.
Ye whose lives are free as sunshine, finding, wheresoe'er ye roam,
Smiles of welcome, looks of kindness, making all the world like home;
In the veins of whose affections kindred blood is but a part,
Of one kindly current throbbing from the universal heart;
Can ye know the deeper meaning of a love in Slavery nursed,
Last flower of a lost Eden, blooming in that Soil accursed?
Love of Home, and Love of Woman! dear to all, but doubly dear
To the heart whose pulses elsewhere measure only hate and fear.
All around the desert circles, underneath a brazen sky,
Only one green spot remaining where the dew is never dry!
From the horror of that desert, from its atmosphere of hell,
Turns the fainting spirit thither, as the diver seeks his bell.
'Tis the fervid tropic noontime; faint and low the sea-waves beat;
Hazy rise the inland mountains through the glimmer of the heat,
Where, through mingled leaves and blossoms, arrowy sunbeams flash and glisten,
Speaks her lover to the slave-girl, and she lifts her head to listen:
'We shall live as slaves no longer! Freedom's hour is close at hand!
Rocks her bark upon the waters, rests the boat upon the strand!
'I have seen the Haytien Captain; I have seen his swarthy crew,
Haters of the pallid faces, to their race and color true.
'They have sworn to wait our coming till the night has passed its noon,
And the gray and darkening waters roll above the sunken moon!'
Oh, the blessed hope of freedom! how with joy and glad surprise,
For an instant throbs her bosom, for an instant beam her eyes!
But she looks across the valley, where her mother's hut is seen,
Through the snowy bloom of coffee, and the lemon-leaves so green.
And she answers, sad and earnest: 'It were wrong for thee to stay;
God hath heard thy prayer for freedom, and his finger points the way.

'Well I know with what endurance, for the sake of me and mine,
Thou hast borne too long a burden never meant for souls like thine.
'Go; and at the hour of midnight, when our last farewell is o'er,
Kneeling on our place of parting, I will bless thee from the shore.
'But for me, my mother, lying on her sick-bed all the day,
Lifts her weary head to watch me, coming through the twilight gray.
'Should I leave her sick and helpless, even freedom, shared with thee,
Would be sadder far than bondage, lonely toil, and stripes to me.
'For my heart would die within me, and my brain would soon be wild;
I should hear my mother calling through the twilight for her child!'
Blazing upward from the ocean, shines the sun of morning-time,
Through the coffee-trees in blossom, and green hedges of the lime.
Side by side, amidst the slave-gang, toil the lover and the maid;
Wherefore looks he o'er the waters, leaning forward on his spade?
Sadly looks he, deeply sighs he: 't is the Haytien's sail he sees,
Like a white cloud of the mountains, driven seaward by the breeze!
But his arm a light hand presses, and he hears a low voice call:
Hate of Slavery, hope of Freedom, Love is mightier than all.

The World's Convention Of The Friends Of Emancipation,
Held In London In 1840
Yes, let them gather! Summon forth
The pledged philanthropy of Earth.
From every land, whose hills have heard
The bugle blast of Freedom waking;
Or shrieking of her symbol-bird
From out his cloudy eyrie breaking:
Where Justice hath one worshipper,
Or truth one altar built to her;
Where'er a human eye is weeping
O'er wrongs which Earth's sad children know;
Where'er a single heart is keeping
Its prayerful watch with human woe:
Thence let them come, and greet each other,
And know in each a friend and brother!
Yes, let them come! from each green vale
Where England's old baronial halls
Still bear upon their storied walls
The grim crusader's rusted mail,
Battered by Paynim spear and brand
On Malta's rock or Syria's sand.!
And mouldering pennon-staves once set
Within the soil of Palestine,
By Jordan and Gennesaret;
Or, borne with England's battle line,
O'er Acre's shattered turrets stooping,
Or, midst the camp their banners drooping,
With dews from hallowed Hermon wet,
A holier summons now is given
Than that gray herinit's voice of old,
Which unto all the winds of heaven

The banners of the Cross unrolled!
Not for the long-deserted shrine;
Not for the dull unconscious sod,
Which tells not by one lingering sign
That there the hope of Israel trod;
But for that truth, for which alone
In pilgrim eyes are sanctified
The garden moss, the mountain stone,
Whereon His holy sandals pressed,
The fountain which His lip hath blessed,
Whate'er hath touched His garment's hem
At Bethany or Bethlehem,
Or Jordan's river-side.
For Freedom in the name of Him
Who came to raise Earth's drooping poor,
To break the chain from every limb,
The bolt from every prison door!
For these, o'er all the earth hath passed
An ever-deepening trumpet blast,
As if an angel's breath had lent
Its vigor to the instrument.
And Wales, from Snowrich's mountain wall,
Shall startle at that thrilling call,
As if she heard her bards again;
And Erin's 'harp on Tara's wall'
Give out its ancient strain,
Mirthful and sweet, yet sad withal,
The melody which Erin loves,
When o'er that harp, 'mid bursts of gladness
And slogan cries and lyke-wake sadness,
The hand of her O'Connell moves!
Scotland, from lake and tarn and rill,
And mountain hold, and heathery hill,
Shall catch and echo back the note,
As if she heard upon the air
Once more her Cameronian's prayer.
And song of Freedom float.
And cheering echoes shall reply
From each remote dependency,
Where Britain's mighty sway is known,
In tropic sea or frozen zone;
Where'er her sunset flag is furling,
Or morning gun-fire's smoke is curling;
From Indian Bengal's groves of palm
And rosy fields and gales of balm,
Where Eastern pomp and power are rolled
Through regal Ava's gates of gold;
And from the lakes and ancient woods
And dim Canadian solitudes,
Whence, sternly from her rocky throne,
Queen of the North, Quebec looks down;
And from those bright and ransomed Isles

Where all unwonted Freedom smiles,
And the dark laborer still retains
The scar of slavery's broken chains!
From the hoar Alps, which sentinel
The gateways of the land of Tell,
Where morning's keen and earliest glance
On Jura's rocky wall is thrown,
And from the olive bowers of France
And vine groves garlanding the Rhone,
'Friends of the Blacks,' as true and tried
As those who stood by Oge's side,
And heard the Haytien's tale of wrong,
Shall gather at that summons strong;
Broglie, Passy, and he whose song
Breathed over Syria's holy sod,
And in the paths which Jesus trod,
And murmured midst the hills which hem
Crownless and sad Jerusalem,
Hath echoes whereso'er the tone
Of Israel's prophey-lyre is known.
Still let them come; from Quito's walls,
And from the Orinoco's tide,
From Lima's Inca-haunted halls,
From Santa Fe and Yucatan,
Men who by swart Guerrero's side
Proclaimed the deathless rights of man,
Broke every bond and fetter off,
And hailed in every sable serf
A free and brother Mexican!
Chiefs who across the Andes' chain
Have followed Freedom's flowing pennon,
And seen on Junin's fearful plain,
Glare o'er the broken ranks of Spain
The fire-burst of Bolivar's cannon!
And Hayti, from her mountain land,
Shall send the sons of those who hurled
Defiance from her blazing strand,
The war-gage from her Petition's hand,
Alone against a hostile world.
Nor all unmindful, thou, the while,
Land of the dark and mystic Nile!
Thy Moslem mercy yet may shame
All tyrants of a Christian name,
When in the shade of Gizeh's pile,
Or, where, from Abyssinian hills
El Gerek's upper fountain fills,
Or where from Mountains of the Moon
El Abiad bears his watery boon,
Where'er thy lotus blossoms swim
Within their ancient hallowed waters;
Where'er is heard the Coptic hymn,
Or song of Nubia's sable daughters;

The curse of slavery and the crime,
Thy bequest from remotest time,
At thy dark Mehemet's decree
Forevermore shall pass from thee;
And chains forsake each captive's limb
Of all those tribes, whose hills around
Have echoed back the cymbal sound
And victor horn of Ibrahim.
And thou whose glory and whose crime
To earth's remotest bound and clime,
In mingled tones of awe and scorn,
The echoes of a world have borne,
My country! glorious at thy birth,
A day-star flashing brightly forth,
The herald-sign of Freedom's dawn!
Oh, who could dream that saw thee then,
And watched thy rising from afar,
That vapors from oppression's fen
Would cloud the upward tending star?
Or, that earth's tyrant powers, which heard,
Awe-struck, the shout which hailed thy dawning,
Would rise so soon, prince, peer, and king,
To mock thee with their welcoming,
Like Hades when her thrones were stirred
To greet the down-east Star of Morning!
'Aha! and art thou fallen thus?
Art thou become as one of us?'
Land of my fathers! there will stand,
Amidst that world-assembled band,
Those owning thy maternal claim
Unweakened by thy crime and shame;
The sad reprovers of thy wrong;
The children thou hast spurned so long.
Still with affection's fondest yearning
To their unnatural mother turning.
No traitors they! but tried and leal,
Whose own is but thy general weal,
Still blending with the patriot's zeal
The Christian's love for human kind,
To caste and climate unconfined.
A holy gathering! peaceful all:
No threat of war, no savage call
For vengeance on an erring brother!
But in their stead the godlike plan
To teach the brotherhood of man
To love and reverence one another,
As sharers of a common blood,
The children of a common God!
Yet, even at its lightest word,
Shall Slavery's darkest depths be stirred:
Spain, watching from her Moro's keep
Her slave-ships traversing the deep,

And Rio, in her strength and pride,
Lifting, along her mountain-side,
Her snowy battlements and towers,
Her lemon-groves and tropic bowers,
With bitter hate and sullen fear
Its freedom-giving voice shall hear;
And where my country's flag is flowing,
On breezes from Mount Vernon blowing,
Above the Nation's council halls,
Where Freedom's praise is loud and long,
While close beneath the outward walls
The driver plies his reeking thong;
The hammer of the man-thief falls,
O'er hypocritic cheek and brow
The crimson flush of shame shall glow
And all who for their native land
Are pledging life and heart and hand,
Worn watchers o'er her changing weal,
Who for her tarnished honor feel,
Through cottage door and council-hall
Shall thunder an awakening call.
The pen along its page shall burn
With all intolerable scorn;
An eloquent rebuke shall go
On all the winds that Southward blow;
From priestly lips, now sealed and dumb,
Warning and dread appeal shall come,
Like those which Israel heard from him,
The Prophet of the Cherubim;
Or those which sad Esaias hurled
Against a sin-accursed world!
Its wizard leaves the Press shall fling
Unceasing from its iron wing,
With characters inscribed thereon,
As fearful in the despot's hall
As to the pomp of Babylon
The fire-sign on the palace wall!
And, from her dark iniquities,
Methinks I see my country rise:
Not challenging the nations round
To note her tardy justice done;
Her captives from their chains unbound,
Her prisons opening to the sun:
But tearfully her arms extending
Over the poor and unoffending;
Her regal emblem now no longer
A bird of prey with talons reeking,
Above the dying captive shrieking,
But, spreading out her ample wing,
A broad, impartial covering,
The weaker sheltered by the stronger!
Oh, then to Faith's anointed eyes

The promised token shall be given;
And on a nation's sacrifice,
Atoning for the sin of years,
And wet with penitential tears,
The fire shall fall from Heaven!

To A Southern Statesman

Is this thy voice whose treble notes of fear
Wail in the wind? And dost thou shake to hear,
Actæon-like, the bay of thine own hounds,
Spurning the leash, and leaping o'er their bounds?
Sore-baffled statesman! when thy eager hand,
With game afoot, unslipped the hungry pack,
To hunt down Freedom in her chosen land,
Hadst thou no fear, that, erelong, doubling back,
These dogs of thine might snuff on Slavery's track?
Where's now the boast, which even thy guarded tongue,
Cold, calm, and proud, in the teeth o' the Senate flung,
O'er the fulfilment of thy baleful plan,
Like Satan's triumph at the fall of man?
How stood'st thou then, thy feet on Freedom planting,
And pointing to the lurid heaven afar,
Whence all could see, through the south windows slanting,
Crimson as blood, the beams of that Lone Star!
The Fates are just; they give us but our own;
Nemesis ripens what our hands have sown.
There is an Eastern story, not unknown,
Doubtless, to thee, of one whose magic skill
Called demons up his water-jars to fill;
Defty and silently, they did his will,
But, when the task was done, kept pouring still.
In vain with spell and charm the wizard wrought,
Faster and faster were the buckets brought,
Higher and higher rose the flood around,
Till the fiends clapped their hands above their master drowned!
So, Carolinian, it may prove with thee,
For God still overrules man's schemes, and takes
Craftiness in its self-set snare, and makes
The wrath of man to praise Him. It may be,
That the roused spirits of Democracy
May leave to freer States the same wide door
Through which thy slave-cursed Texas entered in,
From out the blood and fire, the wrong and sin,
Of the stormed city and the ghastly plain,
Beat by hot hail, and wet with bloody rain,
The myriad-handed pioneer may pour,
And the wild West with the roused North combine
And heave the engineer of evil with his mine.

To Englishmen

You flung your taunt across the wave;
We bore it as became us,
Well knowing that the fettered slave
Left friendly lips no option save
To pity or to blame us.
You scoffed our plea. 'Mere lack of will,
Not lack of power,' you told us:
We showed our free-state records; still
You mocked, confounding good and ill,
Slave-haters and slaveholders.
We struck at Slavery; to the verge
Of power and means we checked it;
Lo! — presto, change! its claims you urge,
Send greetings to it o'er the surge,
And comfort and protect it.
But yesterday you scarce could shake,
In slave-abhorring rigor,
Our Northern palms for conscience' sake:
To-day you clasp the hands that ache
With 'walloping the nigger!'
O Englishmen! — in hope and creed,
In blood and tongue our brothers!
We too are heirs of Runnymede;
And Shakespeare's fame and Cromwell's deed
Are not alone our mother's.
'Thicker than water,' in one rill
Through centuries of story
Our Saxon blood has flowed, and still
We share with you its good and ill,
The shadow and the glory.
Joint heirs and kinfolk, leagues of wave
Nor length of years can part us:
Your right is ours to shrine and grave,
The common freehold of the brave,
The gift of saints and martyrs.
Our very sins and follies teach
Our kindred frail and human:
We carp at faults with bitter speech,
The while, for one unshared by each,
We have a score in common.
We bowed the heart, if not the knee,
To England's Queen, God bless her!
We praised you when your slaves went free:
We seek to unchain ours. Will ye
Join hands with the oppressor?
And is it Christian England cheers
The bruiser, not the bruisëd?
And must she run, despite the tears
And prayers of eighteen hundred years,
Amuck in Slavery's crusade?
Oh, black disgrace! Oh, shame and loss
Too deep for tongue to phrase on!

Tear from your flag its holy cross,
And in your van of battle toss
The pirate's skull-bone blazon!

To George B. Cheever

So spake Esaias: so, in words of flame,
Tekoa's prophet-herdsman smote with blame
The traffickers in men, and put to shame,
All earth and heaven before,
The sacerdotal robbers of the poor.

All the dread Scripture lives for thee again,
To smite like lightning on the hands profane
Lifted to bless the slave-whip and the chain.
Once more the old Hebrew tongue
Bends with the shafts of God a bow new-strung!

Take up the mantle which the prophets wore;
Warn with their warnings, show the Christ once more
Bound, scourged, and crucified in His blameless poor;
And shake above our land
The unquenched bolts that blazed in Hosea's hand!

Not vainly shalt thou cast upon our years
The solemn burdens of the Orient seers,
And smite with truth a guilty nation's ears.
Mightier was Luther's word
Than Seckingen's mailed arm or Hutton's sword!

To James T. Fields

Well thought! who would not rather hear
The songs to Love and Friendship sung
Than those which move the stranger's tongue,
And feed his unselected ear?

Our social joys are more than fame;
Life withers in the public look.
Why mount the pillory of a book,
Or barter comfort for a name?

Who in a house of glass would dwell,
With curious eyes at every pane?
To ring him in and out again,
Who wants the public crier's bell?

To see the angel in one's way,
Who wants to play the ass's part,
Bear on his back the wizard Art,
And in his service speak or bray?

And who his manly locks would shave,
And quench the eyes of common sense,
To share the noisy recompense
That mocked the shorn and blinded slave?

The heart has needs beyond the head,
And, starving in the plenitude
Of strange gifts, craves its common food,
Our human nature's daily bread.

We are but men: no gods are we,
To sit in mid-heaven, cold and bleak,
Each separate, on his painful peak,
Thin-cloaked in self-complacency.

Better his lot whose axe is swung
In Wartburg woods, or that poor girl's
Who by the him her spindle whirls
And sings the songs that Luther sung,

Than his who, old, and cold, and vain,
At Weimar sat, a demigod,
And bowed with Jove's imperial nod
His votaries in and out again!

Ply, Vanity, thy winged feet!
Ambition, hew thy rocky stair!
Who envies him who feeds on air
The icy splendor of his seat?

I see your Alps, above me, cut
The dark, cold sky; and dim and lone
I see ye sitting, stone on stone,
With human senses dulled and shut.

I could not reach you, if I would,
Nor sit among your cloudy shapes;
And (spare the fable of the grapes
And fox) I would not if I could.

Keep to your lofty pedestals!
The safer plain below I choose
Who never wins can rarely lose,
Who never climbs as rarely falls.

Let such as love the eagle's scream
Divide with him his home of ice
For me shall gentler notes suffice,
The valley-song of bird and stream;

The pastoral bleat, the drone of bees,
The flail-beat chiming far away,

The cattle-low, at shut of day,
The voice of God in leaf and breeze;

Then lend thy hand, my wiser friend,
And help me to the vales below,
(In truth, I have not far to go,)
Where sweet with flowers the fields extend.

To John C. Freemont

Thy error, Frémont, simply was to act
A brave man's part, without the statesman's tact,
And, taking counsel but of common sense,
To strike at cause as well as consequence.
Oh, never yet since Roland wound his horn
At Roncesvalles, has a blast been blown
Far-heard, wide-echoed, startling as thine own,
Heard from the van of freedom's hope forlorn!
It had been safer, doubtless, for the time,
To flatter treason, and avoid offence
To that Dark Power whose underlying crime
Heaves upward its perpetual turbulence.
But if thine be the fate of all who break
The ground for truth's seed, or forerun their years
Till lost in distance, or with stout hearts make
A lane for freedom through the level spears,
Still take thou courage! God has spoken through thee,
Irrevocable, the mighty words, Be free!
The land shakes with them, and the slave's dull ear
Turns from the rice-swamp stealthily to hear.
Who would recall them now must first arrest
The winds that blow down from the free Northwest,
Ruffling the Gulf; or like a scroll roll back
The Mississippi to its upper springs.
Such words fulfil their prophecy, and lack
But the full time to harden into things.

To The Memory Of Charles B. Storrs

Thou hast fallen in thine armor,
Thou martyr of the Lord
With thy last breath crying 'Onward!'
And thy hand upon the sword.
The haughty heart derideth,
And the sinful lip reviles,
But the blessing of the perishing
Around thy pillow smiles!

When to our cup of trembling
The added drop is given,
And the long-suspended thunder
Falls terribly from Heaven,

When a new and fearful freedom
Is proffered of the Lord
To the slow-consuming Famine,
The Pestilence and Sword!

When the refuges of Falsehood
Shall be swept away in wrath,
And the temple shall be shaken,
With its idol, to the earth,
Shall not thy words of warning
Be all remembered then?
And thy now unheeded message
Burn in the hearts of men?

Oppression's hand may scatter
Its nettles on thy tomb,
And even Christian bosoms
Deny thy memory room;
For lying lips shall torture
Thy mercy into crime,
And the slanderer shall flourish
As the bay-tree for a time.

But where the south-wind lingers
On Carolina's pines,
Or falls the careless sunbeam
Down Georgia's golden mines;
Where now beneath his burthen
The toiling slave is driven;
Where now a tyrant's mockery
Is offered unto Heaven;

Where Mammon hath its altars
Wet o'er with human blood,
And pride and lust debases
The workmanship of God,
There shall thy praise be spoken,
Redeemed from Falsehood's ban,
When the fetters shall be broken,
And the slave shall be a man!

Joy to thy spirit, brother!
A thousand hearts are warm,
A thousand kindred bosoms
Are baring to the storm.
What though red-handed Violence
With secret Fraud combine?
The wall of fire is round us,
Our Present Help was thine.

Lo, the waking up of nations,
From Slavery's fatal sleep;

The murmur of a Universe,
Deep calling unto Deep!
Joy to thy spirit, brother!
On every wind of heaven
The onward cheer and summons
Of Freedom's voice is given!

Glory to God forever!
Beyond the despot's will
The soul of Freedom liveth
Imperishable still.
The words which thou hast uttered
Are of that soul a part,
And the good seed thou hast scattered
Is springing from the heart.

In the evil days before us,
And the trials yet to come,
In the shadow of the prison,
Or the cruel martyrdom,
We will think of thee, O brother!
And thy sainted name shall be
In the blessing of the captive,
And the anthem of the free.

To The Memory Of Thomas Shipley

Gone to thy Heavenly Father's rest!
The flowers of Eden round thee blowing,
And on thine ear the murmurs blest
Of Siloa's waters softly flowing!
Beneath that Tree of Life which gives
To all the earth its healing leaves
In the white robe of angels clad,
And wandering by that sacred river,
Whose streams of holiness make glad
The city of our God forever!
Gentlest of spirits! not for thee
Our tears are shed, our sighs are given;
Why mourn to know thou art a free
Partaker of the joys of heaven?
Finished thy work, and kept thy faith
In Christian firmness unto death;
And beautiful as sky and earth,
When autumn's sun is downward going,
The blessed memory of thy worth
Around thy place of slumber glowing!
But woe for us! who linger still
With feebler strength and hearts less lowly,
And minds less steadfast to the will
Of Him whose every work is holy.
For not like thine, is crucified

The spirit of our human pride:
And at the bondman's tale of woe,
And for the outcast and forsaken,
Not warm like thine, but cold and slow,
Our weaker sympathies awaken.
Darkly upon our struggling way
The storm of human hate is sweeping;
Hunted and branded, and a prey,
Our watch amidst the darkness keeping,
Oh, for that hidden strength which can
Nerve unto death the inner man!
Oh, for thy spirit, tried and true,
And constant in the hour of trial,
Prepared to suffer, or to do,
In meekness and in self-denial.
Oh, for that spirit, meek and mild,
Derided, spurned, yet uncomplaining;
By man deserted and reviled,
Yet faithful to its trust remaining.
Still prompt and resolute to save
From scourge and chain the hunted slave;
Unwavering in the Truth's defence,
Even where the fires of Hate were burning,
The unquailing eye of innocence
Alone upon the oppressor turning!
O loved of thousands! to thy grave,
Sorrowing of heart, thy brethren bore thee.
The poor man and the rescued slave
Wept as the broken earth closed o'er thee;
And grateful tears, like summer rain,
Quickened its dying grass again!
And there, as to some pilgrim-shrine,
Shall come the outcast and the lowly,
Of gentle deeds and words of thine
Recalling memories sweet and holy!
Oh, for the death the righteous die!
An end, like autumn's day declining,
On human hearts, as on the sky,
With holier, tenderer beauty shining;
As to the parting soul were given
The radiance of an opening heaven!
As if that pure and blessed light,
From off the Eternal altar flowing,
Were bathing, in its upward flight,
The spirit to its worship going!

Toussaint L'Ouverture
'T was night. The tranquil moonlight smile
With which Heaven dreams of Earth, shed down
Its beauty on the Indian isle,
On broad green field and white-walled town;

And inland waste of rock and wood,
In searching sunshine, wild and rude,
Rose, mellowed through the silver gleam,
Soft as the landscape of a dream.
All motionless and dewy wet,
Tree, vine, and flower in shadow met:
The myrtle with its snowy bloom,
Crossing the nightshade's solemn gloom,
The white cecropia's silver rind
Relieved by deeper green behind,
The orange with its fruit of gold,
The lithe paullinia's verdant fold,
The passion-flower, with symbol holy,
Twining its tendrils long and lowly,
The rhexias dark, and cassia tall,
And proudly rising over all,
The kingly palm's imperial stem,.
Crowned with its leafy diadem,
Star-like, beneath whose sombre shade,
The fiery-winged cucullo played!
How lovely was thine aspect, then,
Fair island of the Western Sea!
Lavish of beauty, even whe
Thy brutes were happier than thy men,
For they, at least, were free!
Regardless of thy glorious clime,
Unmindful of thy soil of flowers,
The toiling negro sighed, that Time
No faster sped his hours.
For, by the dewy moonlight still,
He fed the weary-turning mill,
Or bent him in the chill morass,
To pluck the long and tangled grass,
And hear above his scar-worn back
The heavy slave-whip's frequent crack:
While in his heart one evil thought
In solitary madness wrought,
One baleful fire surviving still
The quenching of the immortal mind,
One sterner passion of his kind,
Which even fetters could not kill,
The savage hope, to deal, erelong,
A vengeance bitterer than his wrong!
Hark to that cry! long, loud, and shrill,
From field and forest, rock and hill,
Thrilling and horrible it rang,
Around, beneath, above;
The wild beast from his cavern sprang,
The wild bird from her grove!
Nor fear, nor joy, nor agony
Were mingled in that midnight cry;
But like the lion's growl of wrath,

When falls that hunter in his path
Whose barbed arrow, deeply set,
Is rankling in his bosom yet,
It told of hate, full, deep, and strong,
Of vengeance kindling out of wrong;
It was as if the crimes of years
The unrequited toil, the tears,
The shame and hate, which liken well
Earth's garden to the nether hell
Had found in nature's self a tongue,
On which the gathered horror hung;
As if from cliff, and stream, and glen
Burst on the startled ears of men
That voice which rises unto God,
Solemn and stern, the cry of blood!
It ceased, and all was still once more,
Save ocean chafing on his shore,
The sighing of the wind between
The broad banana's leaves of green,
Or bough by restless plumage shook,
Or murmuring voice of mountain brook.
Brief was the silence. Once again
Pealed to the skies that frantic yell,
Glowed on the heavens a fiery stain,
And flashes rose and fell;
And painted on the blood-red sky,
Dark, naked arms were tossed on high;
And, round the white man's lordly hall,
Trod, fierce and free, the brute he made;
And those who crept along the wall,
And answered to his lightest call
With more than spaniel dread,
The creatures of his lawless beck,
Were trampling on his very neck!
And on the night-air, wild and clear,
Rose woman's shriek of more than fear;
For bloodied arms were round her thrown,
Aan dark cheeks pressed against her own!
Then, injured Afric! for the shame
Of thy own daughters, vengeance came
Full on the scornful hearts of those,
Who mocked thee in thy nameless woes,
And to thy hapless children gave
One choice, pollution or the grave!
Where then was he whose fiery zeal
Had taught the trampled heart to feel,
Until despair itself grew strong,
And vengeance fed its torch from wrong?
Now, when the thunderbolt is speeding;
Now, when oppression's heart is bleeding;
Now, when the latent curse of Time
Is raining down in fire and blood,

That curse which, through long years of crime,
Has gathered, drop by drop, its flood,
Why strikes he not, the foremost one,
Where murder's sternest deeds are done?
He stood the aged palms beneath,
That shadowed o'er his humble door,
Listening, with half-suspended breath,
To the wild sounds of fear and death,
Toussaint L'Ouverture!
What marvel that his heart beat high!
The blow for freedom had been given,
And blood had answered to the cry
Which Earth sent up to Heaven!
What marvel that a fierce delight
Smiled grimly o'er his brow of night,
As groan and shout and bursting flame
Told where the midnight tempest came,
With blood and fire along its van,
And death behind! he was a Man!
Yes, dark-souled chieftain! if the light
Of mild Religion's heavenly ray
Unveiled not to thy mental sight
The lowlier and the purer way,
In which the Holy Sufferer trod,
Meekly amidst the sons of crime;
That calm reliance upon God
For justice in His own good time;
That gentleness to which belongs
Forgiveness for its many wrongs,
Even as the primal martyr, kneeling
For mercy on the evil-dealing;
Let not the favored white man name
Thy stern appeal, with words of blame.
Has he not, with the light of heaven
Broadly around him, made the same?
Yea, on his thousand war-fields striven,
And gloried in his ghastly shame?
Kneeling amidst his brother's blood,
To offer mockery unto God,
As if the High and Holy One
Could smile on deeds of murder done!
As if a human sacrifice
Were purer in His holy eyes,
Though offered up by Christian hands,
Than the foul rites of Pagan lands!

Sternly, amidst his household band,
His carbine grasped within his hand,
The white man stood, prepared and still,
Waiting the shock of maddened men,
Unchained, and fierce as tigers, when
The horn winds through their caverned hill.

And one was weeping in his sight,
The sweetest flower of all the isle,
The bride who seemed but yesternight
Love's fair embodied smile.
And, clinging to her trembling knee,
Looked up the form of infancy,
With tearful glance in either face
The secret of its fear to trace.
'Ha! stand or die!' The white man's eye
His steady musket gleamed along,
As a tall Negro hastened nigh,
With fearless step and strong.
'What, ho, Toussaint!' A moment more,
His shadow crossed the lighted floor.
'Away!' he shouted; 'fly with me,
The white man's bark is on the sea;
Her sails must catch the seaward wind,
For sudden vengeance sweeps behind.
Our brethren from their graves have spoken,
The yoke is spurned, the chain is broken;
On all the hills our fires are glowing,
Through all the vales red blood is flowing!
No more the mocking White shall rest
His foot upon the Negro's breast;
No more, at morn or eve, shall drip
The warm blood from the driver's whip:
Yet, though Tonssaint has vengeance sworn
For all the wrongs his race have borne,
Though for each drop of Negro blood
The white man's veins shall pour a flood;
Not all alone the sense of ill
Around his heart is lingering still,
Nor deeper can the white man feel
The generous warmth of grateful zeal.
Friends of the Negro! fly with me,
The path is open to the sea:
Away, for life!' He spoke, and pressed
The young child to his manly breast,
As, headlong, through the cracking cane,
Down swept the dark insurgent train,
Drunken and grim, with shout and yell
Howled through the dark, like sounds from hell.
Far out, in peace, the white man's sail
Swayed free before the sunrise gale.
Cloud-like that island hung afar,
Along the bright horizon's verge,
O'er which the curse of servile war
Rolled its red torrent, surge on surge;
And he, the Negro champion, where
In the fierce tumult struggled he?
Go trace him by the fiery glare
Of dwellings in the midnight air,

The yells of triumph and despair,
The streams that crimson to the sea!
Sleep calmly in thy dungeon-tomb,
Beneath Besançon's alien sky,
Dark Haytien! for the time shall come,
Yea, even now is nigh,
When, everywhere, thy name shall be
Redeemed from color's infamy;
And men shall learn to speak of thee
As one of earth's great spirits, born
In servitude, and nursed in scorn,
Casting aside the weary weight
And fetters of its low estate,
In that strong majesty of soul
Which knows no color, tongue, or clime,
Which still hath spurned the base control
Of tyrants through all time!
Far other hands than mine may wreathe
The laurel round thy brow of death,
And speak thy praise, as one whose word
A thousand fiery spirits stirred,
Who crushed his foeman as a worm,
Whose step on human hearts fell firm:
Be mine the better task to find
A tribute for thy lofty mind,
Amidst whose gloomy vengeance shone
Some milder virtues all thine own,
Some gleams of feeling pure and warm,
Like sunshine on a sky of storm,
Proofs that the Negro's heart retains
Some nobleness amid its chains,
That kindness to the wronged is never
Without its excellent reward,
Holy to human-kind and ever
Acceptable to God.

Voice Of New England
Up the hillside, down the glen,
Rouse the sleeping citizen;
Summon out the might of men!
Like a lion growling low,
Like a night-storm rising slow,
Like the tread of unseen foe;
It is coming, it is nigh!
Stand your homes and altars by;
On your own free thresholds die.
Clang the bells in all your spires;
On the gray hills of your sires
Fling to heaven your signal-fires.
From Wachuset, lone and bleak,
Unto Berkshire's tallest peak,

Let the flame-tougued heralds speak.
Oh, for God and duty stand,
Heart to heart and hand to hand,
Round the old graves of the land.
Whoso shrinks or falters now,
Whoso to the yoke would bow,
Brand the craven on his brow!
Freedom's soil hath only place
For a free and fearless race,
None for traitors false and base.
Perish party, perish clan;
Strike together while ye can,
Like the arm of one strong man.
Like that angel's voice sublime,
Heard above a world of crime,
Crying of the end of time;
With one heart and with one mouth,
Let the North unto the South
Speak the word befitting both:
'What though Issachar be strong!
Ye may load his back with wrong
Overmuch and over long:
'Patience with her cup o'errun,
With her weary thread outspun,
Murmurs that her work is done.
'Make our Union-bond a chain,
Weak as tow in Freedom's strain
Link by link shall snap in twain.
'Vainly shall your sand-wrought rope
Bind the starry cluster up,
Shattered over heaven's blue cope!
'Give us bright though broken rays,
Rather than eternal haze,
Clouding o'er the full-orbed blaze.
'Take your land of sun and bloom;
Only leave to Freedom room
For her plough, and forge, and loom;
'Take your slavery-blackened vales;
Leave us but our own free gales,
Blowing on our thousand sails.
'Boldly, or with treacherous art,
Strike the blood-wrought chain apart;
Break the Union's mighty heart;
'Work the ruin, if ye will;
Pluck upon your heads an ill
Which shall grow and deepen still.
'With your bondman's right arm bare,
With his heart of black despair,
Stand alone, if stand ye dare!
'Onward with your fell design;
Dig the gulf and draw the line:
Fire beneath your feet the mine:

'Deeply, when the wide abyss
Yawns between your land and this,
Shall ye feel your helplessness.
'By the hearth, and in the bed,
Shaken by a look or tread,
Ye shall own a guilty dread.
'And the curse of unpaid toil,
Downward through your generous soil
Like a fire shall burn and spoil.
'Our bleak hills shall bud and blow,
VInes our rocks shall overgrow,
Plenty in our valleys flow;
'And when vengeance clouds your skies,
Hither shall ye turn your eyes,
As the lost on Paradise!
'We but ask our rocky strand,
Freedom's true and brother band,
Freedom's strong and honest hand;
'Valleys by the slave untrod,
And the Pilgrim's mountain sod,
Blessed of our fathers' God!'

Yorktown

From Yorktown's ruins, ranked and still,
Two lines stretch far o'er vale and hill:
Who curbs his steed at head of one?
Hark! the low murmur: Washington!
Who bends his keen, approving glance,
Where down the gorgeous line of France
Shine knightly star and plume of snow?
Thou too art victor, Rochambeau!
The earth which bears this calm array
Shook with the war-charge yesterday,
Ploughed deep with hurrying hoof and wheel,
Shot-sown and bladed thick with steel;
October's clear and noonday sun
Paled in the breath-smoke of the gun,
And down night's double blackness fell,
Like a dropped star, the blazing shell.
Now all is hushed: the gleaming lines
Stand moveless as the neighboring pines;
While through them, sullen, grim, and slow,
The conquered hosts of England go:
O'Hara's brow belies his dress,
Gay Tarleton's troop rides bannerless:
Shout, from thy fired and wasted homes,
Thy scourge, Virginia, captive comes!
Nor thou alone: with one glad voice
Let all thy sister States rejoice;
Let Freedom, in whatever clime
She waits with sleepless eye her time,

Shouting from cave and mountain wood
Make glad her desert solitude,
While they who hunt her quail with fear;
The New World's chain lies broken here!
But who are they, who, cowering, wait
Within the shattered fortress gate?
Dark tillers of Virginia's soil,
Classed with the battle's common spoil,
With household stuffs, and fowl, and swine,
With Indian weed and planters' wine,
With stolen beeves, and foraged corn,
Are they not men, Virginian born?
Oh, veil your faces, young and brave!
Sleep, Scammel, in thy soldier grave!
Sons of the Northland, ye who set
Stout hearts against the bayonet,
And pressed with steady footfall near
The moated battery's blazing tier,
Turn your scarred faces from the sight,
Let shame do homage to the right!
Lo! fourscore years have passed; and where
The Gallic bugles stirred the air,
And, through breached batteries, side by side,
To victory stormed the hosts allied,
And brave foes grounded, pale with pain,
The arms they might not lift again,
As abject as in that old day
The slave still toils his life away.
Oh, fields still green and fresh in story,
Old days of pride, old names of glory,
Old marvels of the tongue and pen,
Old thoughts which stirred the hearts of men,
Ye spared the wrong; and over all
Behold the avenging shadow fall!
Your world-wide honor stained with shame,
Your freedom's self a hollow name!
Where's now the flag of that old war?
Where flows its stripe? Where burns its star?
Bear witness, Palo Alto's day,
Dark Vale of Palms, red Monterey,
Where Mexic Freedom, young and weak,
Fleshes the Northern eagle's beak;
Symbol of terror and despair,
Of chains and slaves, go seek it there!
Laugh, Prussia, midst thy iron ranks!
Laugh, Russia, from thy Neva's banks!
Brave sport to see the fledgling born
Of freedom by its parent torn!
Safe now is Speilberg's dungeon cell,
Safe drear Siberia's frozen hell:
With Slavery's flag o'er both unrolled,
What of the New World fears the Old?

www.ingramcontent.com/pod-product-compliance
Lightning Source LLC
Chambersburg PA
CBHW052004090426

42741CB00008B/1551